Cultural Atlas for Young People
THE BIBLE

John Rogerson

Facts On File

For Andromeda:

Editorial Director: Graham Bateman
Senior Art Editor: Steve McCurdy
Cartographic Manager: Olive Pearson
Cartographic Editor: Pauline Morrow
Production Director: Clive Sparling
Typesetter: Brian Blackmore

For Lionheart Books:

Managing Editor: Lionel Bender
Art Editor: Ben White
Designer: Malcolm Smythe
Text Editor: Miles Litvinoff
Assistant Editor: Madelaine Samuel

AN ANDROMEDA BOOK

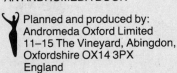 Planned and produced by:
Andromeda Oxford Limited
11–15 The Vineyard, Abingdon,
Oxfordshire OX14 3PX
England

Prepared by Lionheart Books

Library of Congress Cataloging-in-Publication Data

Rogerson, J. W. (John William), 1935–
    The Bible : cultural atlas for young
  people / John Rogerson.
      p.   cm.
    "An Andromeda book"—T.p. verso.
    Includes bibliographical references and
index.
    Summary: Describes the structure,
content, and creation of the Bible; key people
and events in the Old and New Testaments;
and the geographical regions that were
background to those events.
ISBN 0-8160-2908-3
    1. Bible—Antiquities—Juvenile literature.
2. Bible—History of Biblical events—Juvenile
literature.   3. Bible—Geography—Maps.
[1. Bible—History of Biblical events.
2. Bible—Geography.]   I. Title
BS621.R65   1993
220.9—dc20   92-34670

Published in the United States by
Facts On File, Inc.,
460 Park Avenue South,
New York, N.Y. 10016

Facts On File books are available at special
discounts when purchased in bulk quantities for
businesses, associations, institutions or sales
promotions. Please call our Special Sales
Department in New York at 212/683-2244 (dial
800/322-8755 except in NY, AK or HI)

Origination by J. Film Process,
Singapore

Manufactured by New Interlitho
Printed in Italy

10 9 8 7 6 5 4 3 2 1

This book is printed on acid-free paper

CONTENTS

INTRODUCTION

This book is about the history of the Bible and the geography of the lands in which the events it describes took place. It mentions not only the peoples and civilizations of ancient Israel – the Holy Land – but others from around it, such as the Assyrians, Babylonians, and Persians, since they are part of the story. The Bible is a religious work made up of the Old Testament and the New Testament. It contains stories about the creation of the world, legal texts, manuals for priests, records of important events, psalms, proverbs or sayings, love poems, letters, and prophecies or predictions. The Old Testament deals with the history and people of ancient Israel, starting with Abraham, Isaac, and Jacob. The New Testament deals with life and times of Jesus Christ and the rise of Christianity.

The Bible stories about ancient Israel and about Jesus and his followers are set in a land quite different from those we are familiar with today. They were written by many different people, most of whom did not know each other; but each of them expected their readers to know about the lands they described. This atlas is intended to help readers today understand and enjoy the stories in the Bible by opening the door to these lands. It is also the story of a book which for hundreds of years has been the most widely read and bestselling book in the world.

This book will be of interest to two main types of readers. First are those readers who have not been to the Bible Lands and who want to know what their main regions and towns looked like in biblical times. This will help them understand the Bible stories more clearly. Second are those who are visiting Israel and who want a description of each region and an account of the Bible stories that are set there. Within this book are many references to the Bible. Accompanying them are details of where the relevant passages can be found in a complete version of the Bible. Stated first is the name of the book of the Bible, such as Genesis or Proverbs. Next, is the chapter, and finally the verse.

This volume is divided into two main sections. The first, **The History of the Bible Lands**, begins with a short overview of the structure, content, and creation of the Bible. Then it looks in detail at the main stories, characters, peoples, and events described first in the Old Testament and then in the New Testament. Within this section, the articles are arranged chronologically, starting with the story of Abraham and of Moses rescuing the Israelites from Egypt, and ending with the death of Jesus Christ and the work of his disciples. The second section, **The Geography of the Bible Lands**, looks at the landscape of ancient Israel region by region and at some of the more important sites mentioned in the Bible as they are today.

This book is an atlas. There are lots of maps to help you understand what was happening in the Bible Lands at different times. Many of the maps are accompanied by charts giving important dates or useful information. Our story is arranged in double-page spreads. Each spread is a complete story. So you can either read the book from beginning to end or just dip into it to learn about a specific topic. The Glossary on page 92 contains definitions of some of the terms used in the book. If you want to look up a particular place on a map, the Gazetteer on pages 93–94 will tell you where to find it.

▷ A shepherd's life in the Holy Land is almost unchanged since biblical times.

TABLE OF DATES

	7000–2000 BC	2000–1000 BC	1000–900 BC	900–800 BC
HISTORY OF JUDAH, JUDEA, ISRAEL	Pre-pottery new Stone Age tower built at Jericho c.7000 BC.	1750–1550 Abraham travels from Haran to land of Israel. Jacob and his sons settle in Egypt. c.1190 Philistines settle in southern coastal plain. 1220–1020 The Israelites who have left Egypt settle in Bethel and Samaria Hills and Galilee. c.1020 Saul first king of Israel.	1000 BC After the Philistines have killed Saul, David defeats the Philistines and rules over all Israel from Jerusalem. c.961–931 Solomon builds temple in Jerusalem and fortifies many cities. At his death the kingdom divides into Judah (south) and Israel (north).	c.885–874 Omri builds new capital for Israel at Samaria. He controls Judah, Moab, and Edom. The prophets Elijah and Elisha oppose Omri and his son Ahab, and anoint Jehu to destroy their dynasty.
ART AND ARCHITECTURE	Copper 'scepter' from En-gedi, c.3800 BC. Gold helmet from Ur, c.2600 BC.	Clay mask from Hazor, 14th century BC. Burial urn from Jericho, c.18th–16th century BC.	Solomon's temple, 10th century BC. Samarian ivory, 9th century BC.	
HISTORY OF NEIGHBORING PEOPLES IN RELATION TO JUDAH AND ISRAEL	4000–3000 Many new cities established in Mesopotamia. c.2600 Pyramids begin to be built.	Hyksos rule Egypt 1640–1532. Groups such as Jacob and his sons enter Egypt. Sethi I of Egypt (1306–1290) uses the Israelites as slaves. They escape during the reign of Rameses II (1290–1224) led by Moses.	Shoshenq I of Egypt (945–924) invades Judah and Israel.	Shalmaneser III of Assyria (859–824) forces Jehu, king of Israel, to pay tribute in 840.

800–700 BC	700–300 BC	300–100 BC	100 BC–0 AD	0–100 AD

Judah and Israel enjoy peace and prosperity under Uzziah (c.796–767) and Jeroboam II (782–747).

c.760–750 Hosea and Amos condemn social injustices.

722/1 Fall of Samaria and of northern kingdom of Israel.

701 Siege of Jerusalem by Assyrians during reign of Hezekiah (c.727–698).

Judah is subject to Assyria until c.627. Josiah (640–609) regains Judah's independence.

597 Nebuchadnezzar captures Jerusalem and takes 10,000 into exile.

587/6 Nebuchadnezzar destroys the temple.

515 Exiles returning from Babylon build the second temple in Jerusalem.

Alexander the Great's victory at Issus (333) brings Judah under Greek control.

304–198 Judah is part of Ptolemy's Greek kingdom of Egypt.

198 Judah becomes part of Greek kingdom of Syria.

167 Antiochus IV of Syria defiles the Jerusalem temple.

167–164 Maccabean revolt against Antiochus IV.

164–63 Judah ruled by family of Judas Maccabeus.

---

63 Roman general Pompey enters Judah, and begins Roman period.

37–34 Herod the Great made king by Romans. Herod rebuilds the temple, and founds Caesarea and Sebaste, besides much other building work.

?6/4 Birth of Jesus of Nazareth.

28–9 Public ministry of Jesus.

c.30 Crucifixion and Resurrection of Jesus.

33/35 Paul of Tarsus becomes a Christian.

c.47–58 Paul's journeys assist spread of Christianity.

c.61 Paul imprisoned in Rome and later executed.

70 Jerusalem destroyed by Titus.

Cyrus cylinder, c.540 BC.

Tiglath-pileser, an 8th-century BC Assyrian relief.

Lachish letters, c.588 BC.

Alexander the Great at the battle of Issus (333), detail of a mosaic.

Herodium, the citadel built by Herod the Great.

The Jerusalem Menorah AD 70, detail from the Arch of Titus.

Tiglath-pileser III of Assyria (745–727) invades Syria and Israel.
Sargon II (722–705) destroys Samaria.
Sennacherib (705–681) invades Judah in 701.

Decline of Assyria. Its capital Nineveh falls in 612.
Nebuchadnezzar II (605–562) founds Babylonian empire.
Cyrus (559–529) defeats Babylonians and founds Persian empire. Allows Jews to return to Judah.

Alexander the Great (332–323) defeats Persians and establishes an empire from Egypt to borders of India. At his death, the empire is divided among his generals.

Pompey becomes dictator of Rome in 52.
45 Julius Caesar defeats Pompey.
44 Caesar is assassinated.
Octavian (30 BC–AD 14) defeats Mark Antony and becomes emperor.

Nero (54–68) persecutes the Christians.
69–79 Vespasian invades Judea to crush the Jewish revolt of 67–73. His son Titus destroys Jerusalem.

PART ONE

THE HISTORY OF THE BIBLE LANDS

△ Medieval painting depicting Moses on Mount Sinai.

▷ View of the old city of Jerusalem from the southwest. The eight-sided building with the gold dome is the Dome of the Rock, completed in AD 692. It stands on the site of the Jewish temple and is a Muslim shrine in honor of Muhammad's miraculous journey to Jerusalem, from where he went up briefly to heaven. In the left foreground is the open space on the right of which is the western or wailing wall. This wall was built by Herod the Great as part of his enlargement of the temple in the 1st century BC.

WHAT IS THE BIBLE?

The Bible is not so much a book as a library of books. It took over a thousand years to write. It is a religious work made up of two parts, of which the first is the larger. We call this first part the Old Testament and the smaller second part the New Testament.

The Old Testament

The Old Testament was written mostly in the Hebrew language, with a few chapters in Aramaic, another ancient Middle Eastern language. It was written by priests and scribes on parchment (sheepskin or goatskin). It contains 39 sections or "books"; 13 of these are named after prophets (teachers who reminded people about God's commandments).

The stories about the earliest Israelites – Abraham, Isaac, and Jacob – were told out loud from memory. Most of the Old Testament came to be written down and collected together between the 6th and 2nd centuries BC. But some of it is much older, for example poems composed by David in the 11th century BC. The first written alphabet of letters was probably invented during the time of Moses, in the 13th century BC (BC=before Christ).

▽ The 66 books of the Bible. The books contain many types of writing – from creation stories and psalms to gospels and letters. The order shown is that of English Bibles. Hebrew Bibles include only the Old Testament and have a different order, shown here by the color codes. The sequence is The Law, The Former Prophets, The Latter Prophets, The Writings.

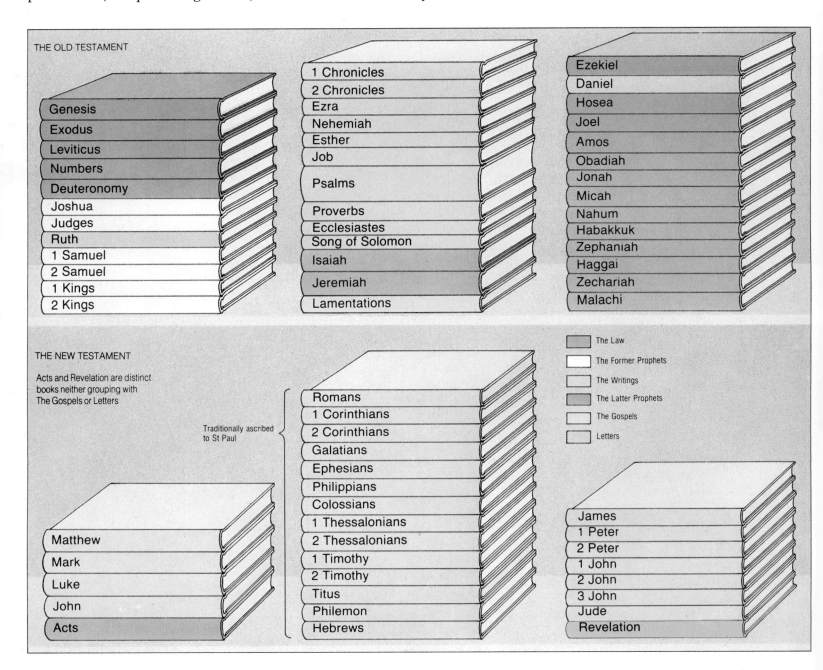

THE OLD TESTAMENT

Genesis
Exodus
Leviticus
Numbers
Deuteronomy
Joshua
Judges
Ruth
1 Samuel
2 Samuel
1 Kings
2 Kings

1 Chronicles
2 Chronicles
Ezra
Nehemiah
Esther
Job
Psalms
Proverbs
Ecclesiastes
Song of Solomon
Isaiah
Jeremiah
Lamentations

Ezekiel
Daniel
Hosea
Joel
Amos
Obadiah
Jonah
Micah
Nahum
Habakkuk
Zephaniah
Haggai
Zechariah
Malachi

THE NEW TESTAMENT

Acts and Revelation are distinct books neither grouping with The Gospels or Letters

Traditionally ascribed to St Paul

Matthew
Mark
Luke
John
Acts

Romans
1 Corinthians
2 Corinthians
Galatians
Ephesians
Philippians
Colossians
1 Thessalonians
2 Thessalonians
1 Timothy
2 Timothy
Titus
Philemon
Hebrews

James
1 Peter
2 Peter
1 John
2 John
3 John
Jude
Revelation

The Law
The Former Prophets
The Writings
The Latter Prophets
The Gospels
Letters

Phonetic value	Early Aramaic	Early Greek
'		
b		
g		
d		
h		
w		
z		
h		
t		
y		
k		
l		
m		
n		
s		
'		
p		
s		
q		
r		
sh		
t		

◁ The earliest known writing used hundreds of signs and goes back to before 3500 BC. But the alphabet was invented later, in the 13th century BC. Aramaic and Greek were influenced by old Hebrew and led to our Roman alphabet. In the Hebrew alphabet some of the signs are related to the names of the letters. The letter "m" is called *mim* in Hebrew, meaning "water"; and you can see ripples in how the letter begins.

▷ Part of Isaiah, written on parchment made from animal skins. Lines that had been left out have been added in smaller script. This is one of the Dead Sea scrolls, written probably in the 1st century BC and found in caves in 1947. Writing materials were expensive in the ancient world, and the earliest writing was done by making marks on clay tablets. Later, papyrus reeds, from Egypt, were used like paper.

The story of the chosen people

The Old Testament tells how God chose the Israelites to be a special people, and how he rescued them from slavery in Egypt. It describes God leading them to their land, and making David their great king, with his capital in Jerusalem. But the Israelites often disobeyed God, despite their prophets' warnings.

Israel's history, from the time of Abraham (about 1750 BC) to the rebuilding of the Jerusalem temple in 515 BC after the Babylonians had destroyed it, is told in Genesis, Exodus, the books of Samuel and Kings, some of the books named after prophets, and the book of Ezra. Other Old Testament books are different. Books such as Job and Ecclesiastes are about the problems of believing in God in a world full of evil. The Psalms are a treasure house of prayers and hymns. And the Song of Solomon contains beautiful love poetry.

The New Testament

The New Testament was the last part of the Bible to be written, in the 1st century AD. It was written in Greek on sheets of paper made from papyrus (a water reed). It has 27 sections or books, most of which are letters written by Paul and his followers to small groups of Christians. The four great Gospels – the books of Matthew, Mark, Luke, and John – describe the life and teachings of Jesus. They were written between AD 70 and 100.

◁ Two scribes, working for the Assyrian king, make lists of goods and prisoners captured in battle. The bearded one uses a clay tablet, while the other writes on papyrus or parchment. The stone carving dates from the 7th century BC.

▷ This tablet from southern Iraq is nearly 5,000 years old. It shows how the earliest writing was in the form of pictures. These then changed as signs began to be used to stand for spoken sounds rather than for things.

ABRAHAM, ISAAC, AND JACOB

The Bible begins by describing God's creation of the world and the first men, women and children. Genesis describes them the way the ancient Hebrews thought of them, not in a modern scientific or historical way. But the stories still have meaning today and give a fascinating picture of the earliest of the Israelites. Abraham, Isaac, and Jacob are known as the patriarchs – the "fathers" of the chosen people of the Old Testament.

Abraham
The history of the Israelites begins with Abraham and his family in Genesis chapter 12. These people moved from place to place with their animals and their possessions in large groups. We have no records of them apart from the Bible. We do not know when Abraham lived, but he and many other people may have migrated through Syria, some of them reaching Egypt in about 1250 BC. The stories about Abraham deal with family matters.

Abraham's ancestors lived in the city of Ur in southern Iraq, a land of great temples known as ziggurats. From Ur, Abraham moved with his father to Haran. Then he stopped being a city-

▽ A reconstruction of a ziggurat built at Ur by Ur-Nammu, king of Ur (2112–2095 BC). The ziggurats were built of brick and had three platforms, on top of which was a temple. Their form may have been partly copied from the pyramids of Egypt, though the pyramids were burial tombs, not temples. The main ceremony held in the ziggurats was probably a sacred marriage between the king – representing the god – and a priestess. Genesis chapter 11 tells the story of the Tower of Babel, possibly connected with a ziggurat in honor of the god Marduk in Babylon.

dweller and traveled south toward the land of Israel. The Bible says Abraham did this because God called him. God promised him that, as a reward, he and his descendants would have a land of their own, Israel.

The Genesis stories tell how a son, Isaac, was born to Abraham and his wife Sarah, and how Isaac escaped from dangers. Abraham finally settled near Hebron and was buried there.

Isaac and Jacob
Isaac acts mainly as a link in the Bible stories between Abraham and his own son, Jacob. He lived mainly in Beer-sheba. Jacob was an ambitious man. After playing a trick on his brother Esau, he fled to Haran, where his grandfather had come from, to escape from Esau's anger. Genesis chapter 32 verses 22 to 32 describes a strange meeting that Jacob had with an angel on his return. This changed him into a better man. He had 12 sons who became the founders of the 12 tribes of Israel.

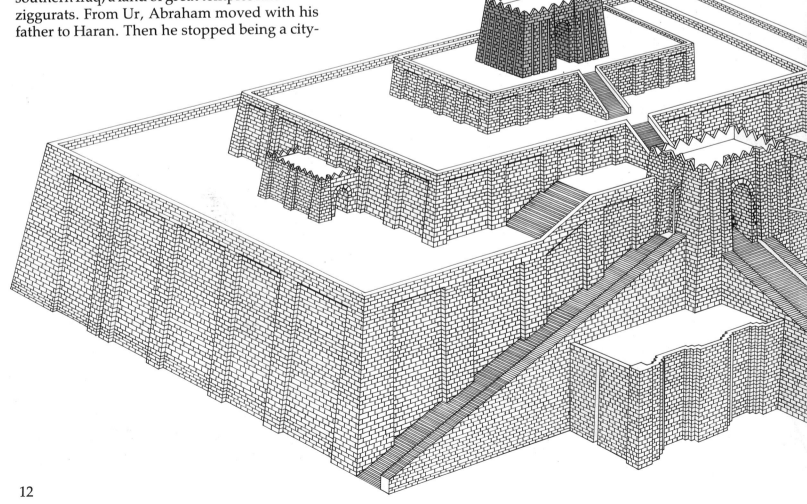

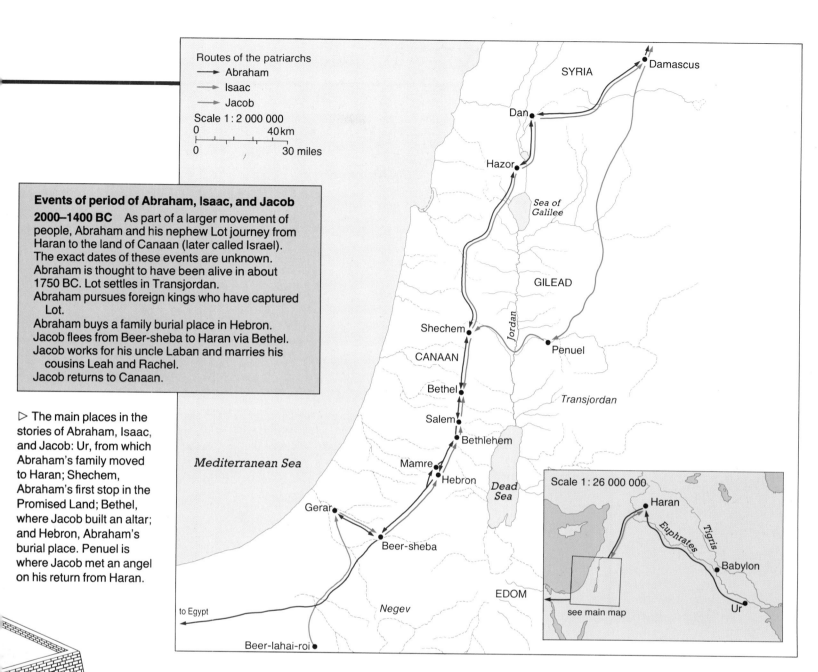

Routes of the patriarchs
→ Abraham
→ Isaac
→ Jacob

Scale 1 : 2 000 000
0   40 km
0   30 miles

SYRIA
Damascus
Dan
Hazor
Sea of Galilee
GILEAD
Jordan
Penuel
Shechem
CANAAN
Bethel
Salem
Bethlehem
Mamre
Hebron
Transjordan
Dead Sea
Mediterranean Sea
Gerar
Beer-sheba
EDOM
Negev
to Egypt
Beer-lahai-roi

Scale 1 : 26 000 000
Haran
Euphrates
Tigris
Babylon
Ur
see main map

Events of period of Abraham, Isaac, and Jacob

2000–1400 BC As part of a larger movement of people, Abraham and his nephew Lot journey from Haran to the land of Canaan (later called Israel). The exact dates of these events are unknown. Abraham is thought to have been alive in about 1750 BC. Lot settles in Transjordan.
Abraham pursues foreign kings who have captured Lot.
Abraham buys a family burial place in Hebron.
Jacob flees from Beer-sheba to Haran via Bethel.
Jacob works for his uncle Laban and marries his cousins Leah and Rachel.
Jacob returns to Canaan.

▷ The main places in the stories of Abraham, Isaac, and Jacob: Ur, from which Abraham's family moved to Haran; Shechem, Abraham's first stop in the Promised Land; Bethel, where Jacob built an altar; and Hebron, Abraham's burial place. Penuel is where Jacob met an angel on his return from Haran.

◁ The mosque in Hebron that stands today on the site of the tomb of Abraham and his wife Sarah. Isaac and Jacob were also buried there. This huge building's foundations were laid by Herod the Great in the 1st century BC. The story of how Abraham bought a cave as a burial place for himself and his family is told in Genesis chapter 23. At last Abraham, who was what we would today call a refugee, owned a part of the land God had promised him. In the picture's foreground are examples of the glassware now made in Hebron.

13

SLAVERY IN EGYPT

Genesis chapters 37 to 48 tell one of the Bible's most exciting stories: the story of Joseph, Jacob's eleventh son and his father's favorite. Joseph is well known for being given a coat of many colors by his father – though the Hebrew may mean "a coat with long sleeves."

The Bible describes how Joseph's brothers disliked him because he had dreams in which he became a ruler over his family. Once, a long way from home with their flocks of sheep and goats, Joseph's brothers sold him to some merchants who were going to Egypt. They pretended to their father that a wild animal had killed Joseph.

Pharaoh's dream

In Egypt, Joseph was sold to a rich man. He did so well that he was soon the manager of all that man's affairs. His master's wife, however, accused Joseph falsely of making love to her, and he was put in prison. There he met two officials of the Pharaoh (the Egyptian king) and was able to tell them the meaning of their dreams.

When Pharaoh had a dream that nobody could interpret, one of the men from prison, now released, remembered Joseph. Joseph successfully explained the meaning of the dream: there would be seven years of good harvests in Egypt followed by seven years of famine. Pharaoh released him from prison and made him a great man in the land.

The Israelites come to Egypt

Because the famine affected Canaan and the family of Jacob, Joseph's brothers went to Egypt to buy grain that had been stored during the good years. Joseph recognized them; but they did not know him. He first played tricks on them but then told them who he was. Jacob and all his family moved to Egypt.

After Joseph died, a new Pharaoh became afraid of the Israelites. He forced them to become slave-laborers, making bricks and building cities.

▷ A servant brings bottles of honey to his Egyptian master. In the early periods of Egyptian history, when a Pharaoh died some of his servants were killed and buried near him so that their spirits could continue to serve him in the afterlife.

▷ This is how the artist Edward Poynter (1836–1919) imagined the slavery of the Israelites in Egypt. Israelite men had short beards on the chin and cheeks. Their tasks were to make bricks and construct buildings. The picture shows both the magnificence of ancient Egypt and the terrible suffering of the Israelite slaves.

How the Israelites became Egypt's slaves

We do not have enough information in the Bible to fit the biblical story with the Egyptian dates. What follows is mostly guesswork.

1750–1550 BC   Egypt ruled by the Hyksos, sometimes called the "shepherd kings."

1550 BC   Expulsion of the Hyksos from Egypt.

?1400 BC   Jacob and his family settle in Egypt, being warned not to call themselves shepherds (Genesis chapter 46 verse 34).

1318–1304 BC   Sethi I founds 19th Dynasty and forces Israelites into slavery. They rebuild cities of Pithom and Raamses (Exodus chapter 1 verse 11).

◁ Slaves throwing grain into the air so that the wind will separate the edible grains from the outer husks. The picture comes from the tomb of Menna in Luxor (Egypt). These were not Israelite slaves: they do not have short beards, and Luxor is far to the south of where the Israelites were settled. The work done by the Israelites was much heavier.

MOSES AND THE EXODUS

The name Moses is Egyptian. Exodus chapter 2 tells us that Moses was a Hebrew who grew up in the court of the Pharaoh. He did not forget his own people, and killed an Egyptian who was beating an Israelite. This forced him to flee for his life. While Moses was living in exile he received a call from God to return to Egypt and to lead the Israelites back to Canaan.

The Passover

The Pharaoh refused to release the Israelites, so God sent plagues to punish the Egyptians. The last and most terrible plague was the death of every firstborn son. The Israelites did not suffer this plague. They marked their houses with the blood of a lamb, so that the destroying angel passed over them. The Jews still celebrate the festival of Passover, remembering how the angel of death spared them.

◁ The traditional route of the Exodus from Pithom and Raamses to Mount Sinai, and then on to Canaan. The wilderness through which the Israelites passed was not a desert of sand, though it was rocky, sandy, and barren. The book of Numbers mentions two routes for the final part of the journey; but both lead northward into Moab to the east of the Dead Sea.

△ Gebel Musa (meaning in Arabic "Mountain of Moses") is thought to be the site of Mount Sinai. It is part of a group of mountains whose highest peak reaches to 8,674ft. Gebel Musa itself is 7,457ft high. While Moses received God's Law on Mount Sinai, the people disobeyed God and made the Golden Calf. Thus the area is a symbol of good and bad.

Map

Scale 1 : 3 700 000

0 — 100km
0 — 80 miles

Mediterranean Sea

CANAAN

Jordan

Lake Manzala

Raamses

Pithom → Succoth
Lake Timsah

Bitter Lakes

EGYPT

Wilderness of Shur

Mt Nebo
Dibon — Mattanah
Dead Sea

Tamar — Iye-abarim

Mt Hor
Kadesh-barnea

Oboth

Punon

Negev

The Arabah

Wilderness of Paran

Timna
Ezion-geber

Marah
Elim

Dophkah

SINAI

MIDIAN

Gulf of Suez

Gulf of Aqaba

Rephidim

Mt Sinai

→ Route of the Exodus
→ Journey into Canaan according to Numbers 21
→ Journey into Canaan according to Numbers 33

From Egypt to the Promised Land

The events of the Exodus are thought to have taken place in the reign of Rameses II. They cannot be dated more exactly than this.

1304–1237 BC Rameses II.

Moses grows up in the Egyptian court, kills an Egyptian who is beating an Israelite, and flees to Midian. Near Mount Sinai he receives God's call to deliver his people. Moses returns to Egypt and demands the freedom of the Israelites. The Pharaoh refuses, and God brings plagues upon the Egyptians.

?1250 BC The Israelites leave Egypt, cross the Sea of Reeds, and travel to Mount Sinai. Moses receives the Ten Commandments from God.

Incident of the Golden Calf.

The Israelites travel toward Canaan.

Moses dies on the borders of Canaan and does not enter the Promised Land.

◁ A bull image used in worship in the ancient Near East. Images such as this one are only about 1ft high. The Golden Calf described in Exodus chapter 32 as being made by the Israelites was probably small if it was made from gold.

▽ An artist's drawing of a Midianite tent shrine discovered at Timna. It is similar to the portable sanctuary described in Exodus chapters 25 to 27 that Moses tells the Israelites to make for the worship of God. The tent shrine shown here dates from a little before the time of Moses. Beneath the covered part was the more holy area, entrance to which may have been restricted to priests. If the Israelite tent shrine was similar, only the covering and the sacred vessels were moved between camps. The walls would be rebuilt at each site.

The Red Sea and Mount Sinai

After the final plague, the Egyptians let the Israelites go – but the Pharaoh then changed his mind and set off after them with his army. We do not know the exact route the Israelites took on leaving Egypt. At some point they came to a place called the Red Sea or possibly the Sea of Reeds. Faced by water ahead and with the Pharaoh's army behind, the Israelites crossed (on dry land), while the Egyptians' heavy chariots became bogged down.

From the Red Sea they traveled slowly to Mount Sinai. Moses climbed the mountain to be closer to God and to receive God's Ten Commandments about how the people were to live and to worship him. These laws, given through Moses, included justice for the weak and the poor. Domestic animals (used for carrying loads and plowing) were also to be treated kindly and, like people, were not to work on the sabbath.

The Golden Calf

The Israelites found the desert hard to cope with. Some even wanted to go back to being slaves in Egypt. Once, while Moses was up the mountain, they decided to make a new god for themselves in the form of a golden calf. This was probably a copy of an Egyptian god. Coming down the mountain, Moses was shocked and saddened at what the people had done.

JOSHUA IN CANAAN

Joshua was appointed by Moses to lead the Israelites into the land of Canaan. They approached the land from the east side of the river Jordan, and after crossing the river they set up a base camp at Gilgal to the north of Jericho.

Joshua's allies

Canaan was home to several peoples, including some relations of Joshua and the Israelites who had not gone to Egypt with Jacob. These people probably joined with Joshua in fighting against the other inhabitants of the land so that the Israelites could settle in peace.

This alliance explains why Joshua only fought battles in the south and the far north, but not in the center of the land. Perhaps the relatives of the Israelites already had some control in these areas. The aim of the Israelite attacks on cities was not to occupy them but to stop them from being a danger in the areas where they wanted to settle.

▷ The conquests of Joshua in Canaan. It is clear that Joshua fought only in certain parts of the land. Of course, the information in the book of Joshua may not be complete. Or the central part of the land may already have been under the influence of peoples related to the Israelites who joined with Joshua.

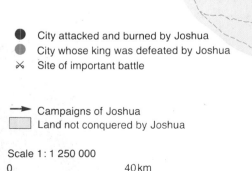

Victory and defeat in Canaan

We do not have enough information in the Bible to date any of the events of Joshua's campaigns.
?1250–1200 BC   Israelites enter Canaan from Transjordan and begin to create space for settlement by attacking Canaanite cities. They possibly link up with other Israelites who did not go down to Egypt.
c.1230 BC   Israel mentioned in the stela (stone column) of Merneptah – the first recorded use of the name Israel outside the Bible. Merneptah (1236–1223 BC) was an Egyptian king who invaded Canaan and set up a monument listing the peoples defeated, including the Israelites.

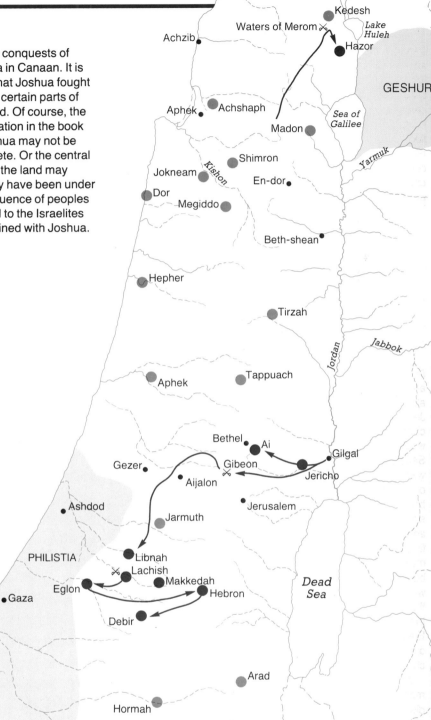

● City attacked and burned by Joshua
● City whose king was defeated by Joshua
✕ Site of important battle

→ Campaigns of Joshua
　 Land not conquered by Joshua

Scale 1 : 1 250 000

0　　　　　　40 km

0　　　　　　　　　30 miles

▷ A tower built in the ancient city of Jericho in about 7000 BC. The tower's purpose was defense either against human enemies or against floods. Its great age is a reminder that the events of the Bible are recent compared with the whole of human history.

▷ A Canaanite charioteer and soldier stand alongside the walls of Jericho. The horse-drawn chariot was a formidable weapon in ancient warfare. Saddles that enabled warriors to ride and fight on horseback had not yet been invented. The chariot sometimes also contained another one or two fighters, including a marksman armed with a bow and arrows. Although we do not know where these horses were bred, the Bible often mentions Egypt as the main source of supply for horses and chariots.

Jericho is one of the most ancient cities so far discovered. It was occupied in about 10,000 BC. It was set in the hot Jordan valley but had a water supply in the form of a spring. The city was destroyed and rebuilt many times. When it was not occupied, heavy rains washed away some of the remains of former cities on the site. Remains of the city described in the book of Joshua have not been found.

The Israelites' battle tactics

The Canaanites were better armed and better equipped than the Israelites. They had horses and chariots, unlike Joshua and his army. The Israelites were unable to gain many victories in places where chariots could be used. They concentrated instead on areas suited to foot soldiers and used surprise tactics.

Describing Joshua's defeat of the city of Hazor in the north, the Bible tells us (Joshua chapter 11 verse 7) that he came suddenly upon the horses and chariots of the enemy. The Israelites probably surprised the army of Hazor while it was camped at the foot of some steep hills, from which Joshua's men rushed down.

Help from God

In the biblical stories Joshua's victories are presented to emphasize the way the Israelites believed that God helped them. At the battle of Jericho the Israelites were told to carry the Ark of the Covenant (a portable sign of God's presence) around the outside of the city for six days. On the seventh day they carried the Ark around seven times; the seventh time, the city walls fell down when trumpets were blown.

In the battle against Ai (whose name means "a ruin"), the Israelites were defeated because they had not obeyed God. So these stories are more about obedience to God than about war.

SAUL AND THE PHILISTINES

During the 13th century BC the Philistines left their homes in Crete and Asia Minor (modern Turkey) and traveled toward Canaan and Egypt. Some came by land and some by sea. The Egyptians – who called the Philistines "sea peoples" – fought them off.

The Philistines in Israel

In the land of Israel (as we shall now call Canaan) the Philistines settled on the coastal plain, mainly in five (later six) cities. For over 150 years the Israelites and Philistines did not trouble each other, but in about 1030 BC the Philistines began to expand. Their soldiers were better organized and, unlike the Israelites, used horses, chariots, and iron weapons. The Israelites' weapons were bronze.

The Philistines forced the Israelite tribe of Dan to leave its territory and settle in the far north. The stories of Samson in the book of Judges belong to this period. The Philistines must also have fought with the tribe of Judah, but we have only hints of this in the Bible. Next they defeated the tribes of Benjamin and Ephraim living in the Bethel and Samaria Hills and took over their land.

The Israelites hoped that the Ark of the Covenant would bring victory. But some of the priests had acted wickedly, and, the Bible says, God allowed the Ark to be captured.

King Saul, Israel's first king

Samuel and his groups of prophets led Israelite resistance. Saul was connected with them. Samuel anointed Saul king (anointing was a ceremony using oil or ointment). We do not know how long Saul reigned, or how and when he became king. However, helped by his son Jonathan, he drove the Philistines from the Bethel and Samaria Hills, and defeated other enemies too.

Saul was brave and religious, and tried to banish bad forms of religion from Israel. He gave the Israelites a period of relief from the attacks of their enemies. But when the Philistines gathered to attack again, Saul was worried and unhappy; he suspected Jonathan and his armor bearer David of plotting against him. David had to run away. Saul and his sons were defeated and killed by the Philistines near Mount Gilboa.

△ This Philistine stone coffin (sarcophagus) from about the 10th century BC was used to contain and preserve the dead. It has human features. We know little about the religion of the Philistines. They seem to have taken over parts of the religion of the other Canaanites.

▷ This dagger made of gold was found at Gezer, at one time one of the Philistine cities. It is a religious object in the form of a goddess and is not a weapon.

◁ Part of a collection of 8th-century BC clay figures probably representing the goddess Astarte. The figures were found on the coastal plain.

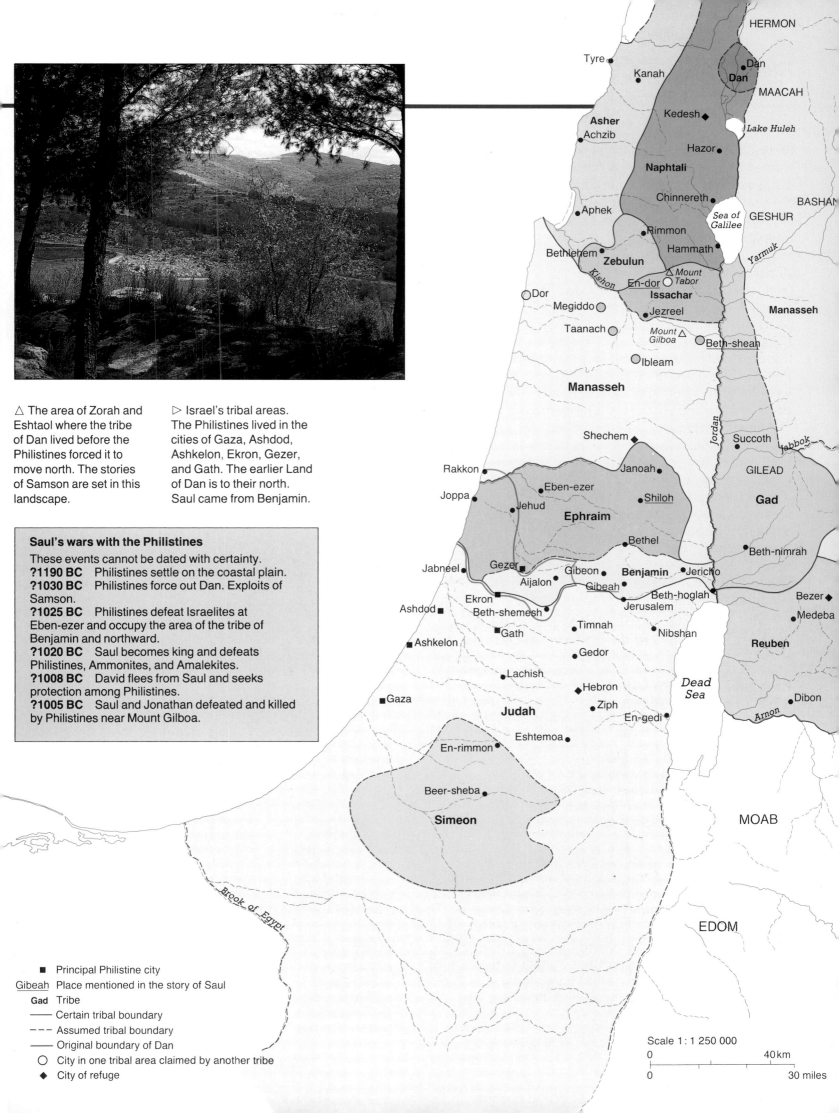

△ The area of Zorah and Eshtaol where the tribe of Dan lived before the Philistines forced it to move north. The stories of Samson are set in this landscape.

▷ Israel's tribal areas. The Philistines lived in the cities of Gaza, Ashdod, Ashkelon, Ekron, Gezer, and Gath. The earlier Land of Dan is to their north. Saul came from Benjamin.

Saul's wars with the Philistines

These events cannot be dated with certainty.
?1190 BC Philistines settle on the coastal plain.
?1030 BC Philistines force out Dan. Exploits of Samson.
?1025 BC Philistines defeat Israelites at Eben-ezer and occupy the area of the tribe of Benjamin and northward.
?1020 BC Saul becomes king and defeats Philistines, Ammonites, and Amalekites.
?1008 BC David flees from Saul and seeks protection among Philistines.
?1005 BC Saul and Jonathan defeated and killed by Philistines near Mount Gilboa.

■ Principal Philistine city
<u>Gibeah</u> Place mentioned in the story of Saul
Gad Tribe
——— Certain tribal boundary
- - - Assumed tribal boundary
——— Original boundary of Dan
○ City in one tribal area claimed by another tribe
◆ City of refuge

Scale 1: 1 250 000
0   40km
0   30 miles

DAVID'S EMPIRE

When Saul was killed in battle, Israel's position seemed hopeless. Yet only about 10 years later the Israelites had cleared the Philistines from the land, had defeated several neighboring peoples, and had created a small empire. One man, David, was largely responsible for this.

David's rise to power

David had joined Saul's army as the king's armor bearer and had become close friends with Jonathan, Saul's eldest son. David's wide popularity made Saul deeply jealous of him, and eventually he was forced to run away. For a time he lived the life of an outlaw, leading a small band of very tough men; then he lived under the protection of the Philistines for a year or so. During this time he built up a small army by raiding peoples to the south of Judah. After Saul's death David convinced the Israelites that he was on their side. He became king of Judah with his capital in Hebron.

The Philistines suspected nothing. Saul's commander, Abner, had set up a remaining son of Saul as king in Transjordan. But after this son and Abner had been betrayed and killed, the remaining Israelite tribes asked David to be their king. He captured Jerusalem, making it the capital of his land, defeated the Philistines, and freed the people from Philistine rule. He then conquered the neighboring peoples of Moab, Ammon, Edom, and Aram (Syria).

◁ The site of the city of David as seen today. The spur – in the bottom right and center of the photograph – is outside the walls of Jerusalem. To its north is the Dome of the Rock, the sacred Muslim shrine built in AD 692 after Jerusalem fell to the Muslims in AD 638.

▷ David's empire. The territory of Israel included sizable areas to the east of the river Jordan. The Philistines still occupied the coastal plain west of Judah; but their "vassal" (dependent) kingdom, like that of Syria in the north, came under David's rule. The conquest of Edom opened up a route via the Gulf of Aqaba and so to parts of Africa and Arabia (though not all routes had roads). It also gave the Israelites control of the copper mines at Timna. Solomon, David's son, made good use of the new trading possibilities.

▷ Jerusalem in David's time was built on a small spur or ridge, overlooked by the surrounding hills, that could be attacked from the north. But it was on the only hill in the area to have a water supply in the form of a permanent spring. David rebuilt Jerusalem and its city walls. At the northern end, where the spur joined the higher ground, was a citadel protecting the city from attack. Solomon built his temple (the tall building on the far right) on the hill to the north of David's city.

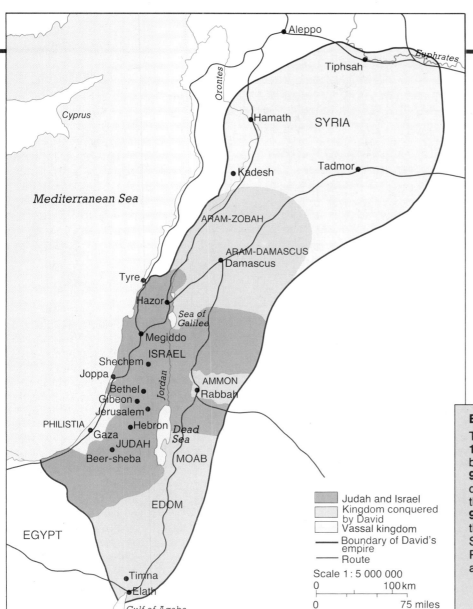

David's later years

The last part of David's reign was less successful. David, surrounded by a bodyguard of non-Israelites, no longer understood his people well. First the people of Judah, led by David's son Absalom, rebelled against him; then the people of the northern tribes revolted. These revolts were crushed, but they were a warning of dangers ahead.

Despite the later problems, the writers of the biblical books of Samuel ended their account of David not with his failures but with his remarkable achievements. He was a gifted musician and a brave and brilliant soldier. He saved his people from a hopeless situation and established them as a nation that would outlast many attempts to destroy it.

Events in the life of David

These events can only be dated approximately.
1000 BC Death of Saul. David moves to Hebron and becomes king of Judah.
992 BC Now king of the remaining tribes, David captures Jerusalem and makes it his capital. He defeats the Philistines.
992–961 BC David defeats Edom, Moab, Ammon, and the Syrian kingdoms. He marries Bath-sheba, to whom Solomon is born.
Revolts of Absalom his son, and of Sheba, son of Bichri, a distant relative of Saul.

Map legend:
- Judah and Israel
- Kingdom conquered by David
- Vassal kingdom
- Boundary of David's empire
- Route

Scale 1 : 5 000 000

0   100 km
0   75 miles

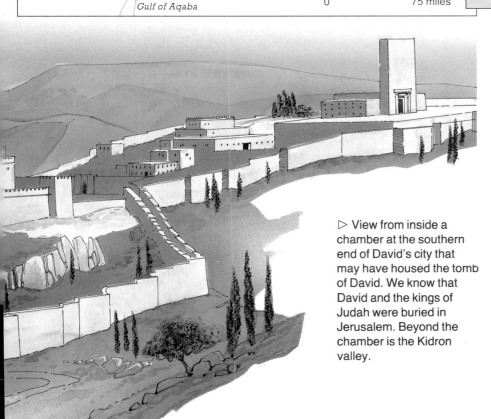

▷ View from inside a chamber at the southern end of David's city that may have housed the tomb of David. We know that David and the kings of Judah were buried in Jerusalem. Beyond the chamber is the Kidron valley.

SOLOMON AND HIS BUILDINGS

When David died, there were two rivals to succeed him as king. These were his sons Adonijah and Solomon. (Another son, the rebel Absalom, had died leading his unsuccessful revolt.) After a brief struggle Solomon won and took control of David's empire.

Solomon established links with neighboring peoples, especially the inhabitants of Tyre and Sidon (northern coastal cities, now both in Lebanon) who were great seafarers and traders. He built a fleet of ships, which sailed from the Gulf of Aqaba to trade with Africa and Arabia. Solomon also exploited the mines in the south of Edom.

Solomon's temple

Solomon was a thoughtful and cultured man who gained a reputation as a composer of proverbs (wise sayings) and songs. His court had an expensive lifestyle. He had great storehouses and an army of charioteers. As the wealth of his kingdom grew, Solomon was determined to make the cities of his kingdom look impressive.

Solomon's most famous building project was the temple he built on the hill to the north of Jerusalem. The hill came to be known as Mount Zion. The Israelites had no experience in designing and building temples and palaces. Solomon therefore entrusted the work to Hiram, king of Tyre.

To build the temple, wood from cedar and cypress trees was imported from the north. The blocks of stone were quarried in Israel by men who were forced into labor gangs. Much of the woodwork in the temple was overlaid with gold, and it must have looked very splendid.

Solomon's other projects

The temple was only one of Solomon's projects. The Bible tells us (in 1 Kings chapters 6 and 7) that the temple took seven years to build, but the king's own palace took 13 years. Solomon enlarged Jerusalem and fortified the southern city of Beer-sheba.

We also learn in the Bible (1 Kings chapter 9 verses 15 to 19) that Solomon rebuilt and fortified many other towns. These included Hazor, Megiddo, and Gezer. Modern excavations have confirmed this. He probably set up forts and outposts to protect his trading routes.

△ A reconstruction of the main hall of Solomon's temple based on the information given in 1 Kings chapter 6 verses 2 to 38. This building had an entrance hall leading to the main hall, with the holy place at the far end. It was surrounded by open-air courtyards where people prayed. Only priests were allowed to enter the most sacred parts of the building.

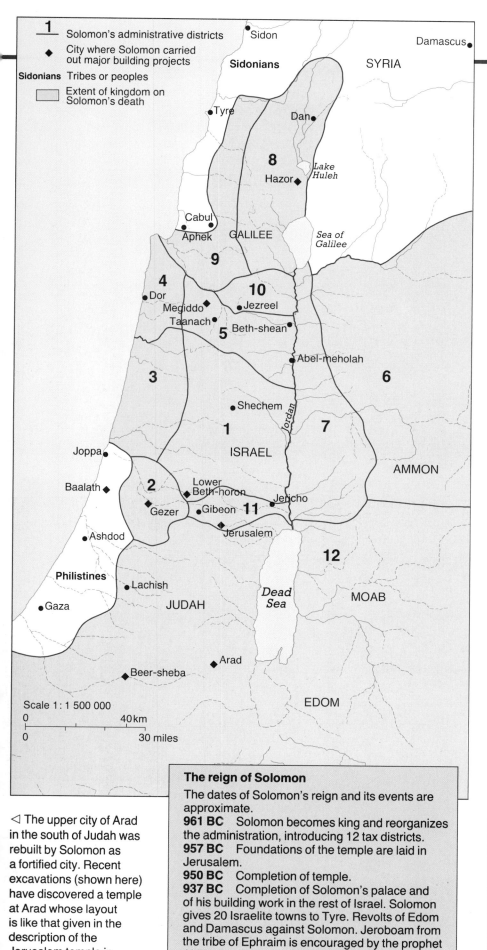

Sidon

Damascus

SYRIA

Sidonians

Tyre

Dan

8

Lake Huleh

Hazor

Cabul

Aphek

GALILEE

Sea of Galilee

9

4

Dor

10

Megiddo

Jezreel

Taanach

5

Beth-shean

3

Abel-meholah

6

Shechem

Jordan

1

ISRAEL

7

Joppa

AMMON

2

Lower Beth-horon

Gezer

Gibeon

11

Jericho

Baalath

Jerusalem

Ashdod

12

Lachish

Dead Sea

MOAB

Philistines

Gaza

JUDAH

Arad

Scale 1 : 1 500 000

Beer-sheba

0   40km

0   30 miles

EDOM

Paying the price

For all this work there was a price to pay. Solomon did not have enough gold and silver to meet the full cost of his ambitious building program, and he was forced to give 20 Israelite towns in Galilee to Hiram. He also divided the land into 12 main administrative districts (for taxation) and made the people provide food for his court and officials.

The Bible says that Solomon forced only non-Israelites into the labor gangs for the building projects. But even if this is true, Solomon's reign took away much of the freedom that villages and towns had enjoyed before as described in Joshua chapters 13 to 19.

◁ The focal points of Solomon's administrative or tax districts and the cities mentioned in the Bible as those where he carried out building projects. Excavations show that other Israelite cities were also rebuilt at this time.

▽ Solomon extended the boundaries of Jerusalem within new walls. His work took place to the right-hand side of the plan, affecting the spur to the bottom right and the area above it. The other walls shown are later additions by various peoples.

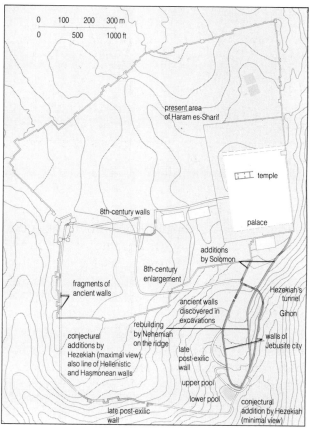

present area of Haram es-Sharif

temple

palace

8th-century walls

additions by Solomon

8th-century enlargement

Hezekiah's tunnel

fragments of ancient walls

ancient walls discovered in excavations

Gihon

conjectural additions by Hezekiah (maximal view); also line of Hellenistic and Hasmonean walls

rebuilding by Nehemiah on the ridge

walls of Jebusite city

late post-exilic wall

upper pool

lower pool

late post-exilic wall

conjectural addition by Hezekiah (minimal view)

◁ The upper city of Arad in the south of Judah was rebuilt by Solomon as a fortified city. Recent excavations (shown here) have discovered a temple at Arad whose layout is like that given in the description of the Jerusalem temple in 1 Kings chapter 6.

The reign of Solomon
The dates of Solomon's reign and its events are approximate.
961 BC Solomon becomes king and reorganizes the administration, introducing 12 tax districts.
957 BC Foundations of the temple are laid in Jerusalem.
950 BC Completion of temple.
937 BC Completion of Solomon's palace and of his building work in the rest of Israel. Solomon gives 20 Israelite towns to Tyre. Revolts of Edom and Damascus against Solomon. Jeroboam from the tribe of Ephraim is encouraged by the prophet Ahijah to rebel. He flees for refuge to Egypt.

ISRAEL AND JUDAH DIVIDE

Judah and the tribes to the north had never been completely united. David first became king over Judah – a rival to what remained of Saul's kingdom. Then the northern tribes asked David to be their king also. David later had to put down a revolt of the northern tribes, and trouble began again in Solomon's reign.

How the division arose

The people in the north disliked the power of Judah and Jerusalem in the south. They had been heavily taxed to pay for Solomon's building projects. Many people also believed that God did not need a permanent temple, and certainly not one in Solomon's capital.

Solomon's son Rehoboam went to Shechem – a city associated with Abraham, Jacob, and Joshua – to meet the northern tribes. But he refused their request to reduce their taxes. Ten of the tribes then rebelled, led by Jeroboam. Only Benjamin remained with Judah.

◁ Samaria, where Omri built his new capital for the northern kingdom of Israel. It was a great site, and so well defended that the Assyrians had to besiege the city for three years before it fell in 722–1 BC. Herod the Great rebuilt it in the 1st century BC and named it Sebaste. Here are remains of the time.

△ An ivory carving of a sphinx (a mythical winged beast) in a lotus thicket – from Omri's royal palace in Samaria. The 9th-century BC palace was richly decorated with such carvings.

◁ The modern Arab village of Beitin on the site of the ancient city of Bethel. Jeroboam set up a sanctuary (sacred place) after he had led the rebellion against Judah.

▽ The two kingdoms of Israel and Judah. Shoshenq, king of Egypt, invaded in about 924 BC. During the 9th century BC, under Omri's rule, Israel controlled Moab and had power over Judah. Later, in the reign of Jehu, Ben-hadad of Syria (the kingdom to the north of Israel, capital Damascus) besieged the Israelite capital of Samaria.

Omri, Ahab, and Jezebel

Soon after the split, the land was invaded by Shoshenq I of Egypt (called Shishak in 1 Kings chapter 14 verse 25). He destroyed many of Solomon's fortified cities and weakened the two kingdoms. In 885 BC King Omri came to power in Israel after a bitter civil war. He established a new capital at Samaria and, with his son Ahab, fortified important Israelite cities. He extended his power over neighboring nations including Judah. He is referred to several times in texts other than the Bible, and after his death the Assyrians still referred to Israel as "Omri-land."

Ahab's wife, the foreign princess Jezebel, tried to introduce her religion into Israel, but she was opposed by prophets led by Elijah and Elisha. After Ahab's death the prophets helped Jehu overthrow the house of Omri and restore worship of the God of Israel. During Jehu's reign, however, Israel was often invaded by the Syrians. Jehu had also to send tribute to the Assyrian king Shalmaneser III (see page 28).

Warnings of the prophets

From about 800 to 750 BC the two kingdoms of Judah and Israel enjoyed new peace and prosperity. But rich citizens had begun to grow wealthy at the expense of the poor. Also, many people turned from the God of Israel to the storm-god Baal. The first of the 8th-century BC prophets, Hosea and Amos, appeared. They warned the people that God would punish them if they continued to worship other gods and to oppress the poor. To the north, the empire of Assyria was preparing to expand down into Syria and Israel.

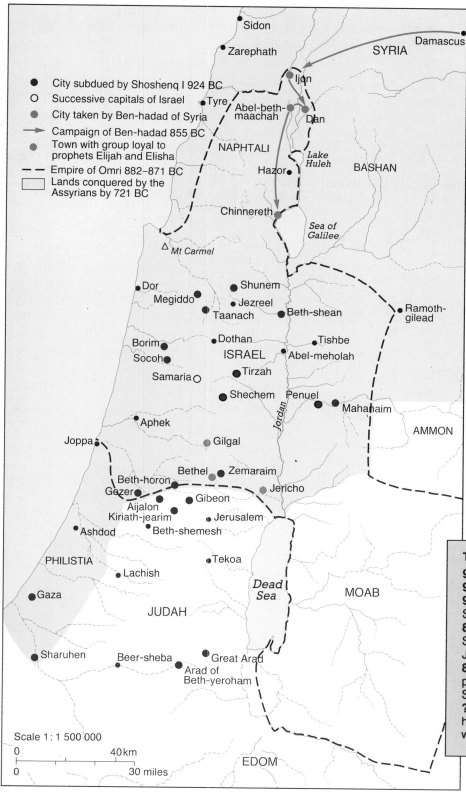

Scale 1 : 1 500 000

- ● City subdued by Shoshenq I 924 BC
- ○ Successive capitals of Israel
- ● City taken by Ben-hadad of Syria
- → Campaign of Ben-hadad 855 BC
- ● Town with group loyal to prophets Elijah and Elisha
- – – Empire of Omri 882–871 BC
- ▢ Lands conquered by the Assyrians by 721 BC

The two kingdoms, 931–750 BC

931 BC Death of Solomon and division of the kingdom.
931–910 BC Jeroboam king of Israel.
924 BC Israel and Judah invaded by Egyptian king Shoshenq I (945–924 BC).
885–874 BC Omri king of Israel. Builds new capital at Samaria, conquers Moab, and extends power over Judah.
873–853 BC Ahab king of Israel is opposed by prophets led by Elijah and Elisha. Dies fighting the Syrians at Ramoth-gilead.
?792–742 BC Uzziah king of Judah. Toward the end of his reign and that of Jeroboam II of Israel, Hosea and Amos warn the peoples of Israel and Judah to return to God.

THE ASSYRIAN CONQUERORS

The land of Assyria was named after the city of Ashur, beside the river Tigris in Mesopotamia (modern Iraq). People lived in Ashur by 2400 BC, and it became the center of an empire in the 14th century BC. Other Assyrian cities, such as Nineveh, were also important.

Defeat of Jehu

The Assyrian king Shalmaneser III (859–824 BC) fought a group of small nations including Ahab's Israel at the battle of Qarqar (853 BC). This battle had no clear winner. But in 841 BC Shalmaneser won a firm victory over Jehu, king of Israel, among others.

Shalmaneser set up an obelisk (a four-sided stone pillar) to mark his victory. It records his military campaigns and other victories, but also shows King Jehu paying tribute to him. Known as the Black Obelisk, this pillar was

found at ancient Kalhu and is the most complete one yet found. In about 800 BC the Assyrians defeated the army of the city of Damascus. This stopped the Syrians raiding Israel. Israel and Judah then enjoyed 50 years of peace and prosperity.

Tiglath-pileser III

Under King Tiglath-pileser III (745–727 BC), called Pul in the Bible, the Assyrian armies overran Syria and Israel. The Assyrians forced some of the peoples they conquered to move to Assyria to work or serve as soldiers. In about 734 BC the kings of Damascus and Israel tried to

▽ The Assyrian empire in the late 8th century BC. A network of main roads, with evenly spaced resting-houses and places to feed or change horses, linked the main towns. Israel was at the extreme southwest of Assyrian lands, and the border with Judah marked their limit. Although Judah stayed outside the empire, the Assyrians had power over it from about 733 to 650 BC.

How Assyrian power grew

853 BC Battle of Qarqar between Shalmaneser III and small nations including Israel.
841 BC Jehu, king of Israel, defeated by Shalmaneser.
745–727 BC Assyrians overrun Syria and Israel.
722–721 BC Sargon II destroys Samaria.
701 BC Jerusalem besieged by Sennacherib. Judah under Assyrian control until 650 BC.

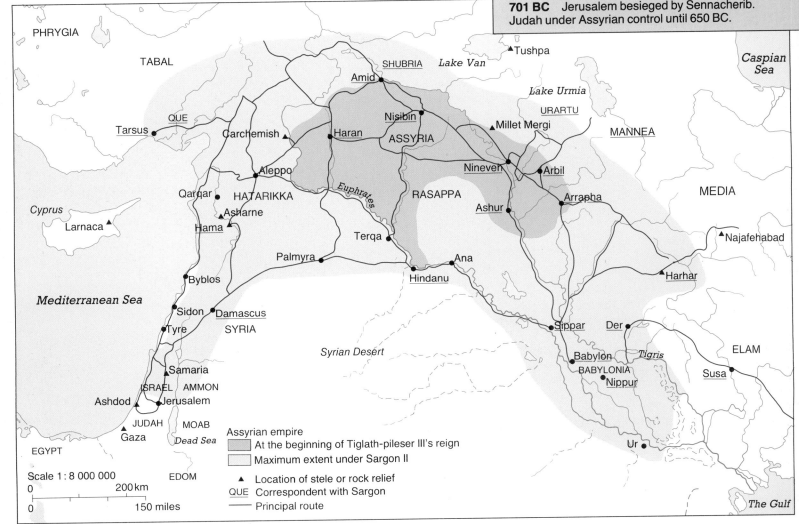

Assyrian empire
▨ At the beginning of Tiglath-pileser III's reign
☐ Maximum extent under Sargon II

▲ Location of stele or rock relief
QUE Correspondent with Sargon
— Principal route

Scale 1 : 8 000 000
0 ___ 200 km
0 ___ 150 miles

force Ahaz, king of Judah, to join them as allies. Ahaz refused and asked the Assyrians for help. In reply, Tiglath-pileser defeated Damascus and seized much of Israel.

What remained of Israel rebelled in about 725 BC, but in 722–721 BC the Assyrians under Sargon II captured Samaria. This meant the end of Israel as an independent kingdom. Only Judah remained.

Hezekiah's rebellion

Several years later Hezekiah, king of Judah, joined a revolt against the Assyrian king Sennacherib. The Assyrians marched against Judah in 701 BC. All the cities of Judah were captured except for Jerusalem. But Hezekiah had to hand over a large sum of money, and the Assyrians controlled Judah for much of the next 80 years.

△ A reconstruction of part of the walls of Nineveh, whose total length was about 7½ mi. The walls were built of stone, with towers at regular intervals. Behind these walls was a second line of fortifications built of bricks.

△ Site plan of Nineveh. This city became the Assyrian capital during the reign of Sennacherib (705–681 BC). Sennacherib built new city walls with 15 gates, as well as a royal palace overlooking the river Khosr.

▷ The Assyrians used machines such as these to capture fortified cities. The machines protected the soldiers who used a battering ram to knock a hole in the walls. The scaling ladders helped to occupy the attention of the defenders. Their successful siege of the Israelite capital Samaria took three years. They were skillful in many areas of warfare.

NEBUCHADNEZZAR, KING OF BABYLON

For most of the 7th century BC Judah, the southern Israelite kingdom, was controlled by Assyria. During the reign of the Judean king Manasseh (699–643 BC) there was much injustice and cruelty. After Manasseh's death his son Amon reigned for only two years before he was killed. Then Amon's eight-year-old son Josiah became king in 640 BC.

Ashurbanipal (669–627 BC) was the last great king of Assyria. He reconquered Egypt. When he died Josiah began to make Judah more independent of Assyria.

The rise of Babylon

Babylon was a city in the southern part of the Assyrian empire. When Ashurbanipal died a Babylonian named Nabopolassar began to build his own empire. In 612 BC he captured and destroyed Nineveh. The Assyrians made a last stand against Babylon at Haran. In 609 BC Josiah of Judah was killed by the Egyptian Neco (Necho II) as he tried to stop the Egyptians going to help the Assyrians. The Assyrians could not hold out, and Babylon triumphed.

Nebuchadnezzar

Nabopolassar died in 605 BC and was followed as king by his son Nebuchadnezzar. He had already defeated the Egyptians at the battle of Carchemish. After his coronation he began the conquest of Syria, Judah, and Egypt.

In 597 BC Nebuchadnezzar captured Jerusalem. King Jehoiachin, who was only 18 and had ruled Judah for only three months, was sent to Babylon as his prisoner. Many other leading Israelites were also taken into exile.

Jehoiachin's uncle, Zedekiah, was put on Judah's throne. After some years he rebelled against Nebuchadnezzar. Babylon marched against Judah in 588 BC. After a siege lasting almost 18 months the Babylonians captured Jerusalem toward the end of the summer of 587 (or 586) BC. The temple built by Solomon was destroyed; all the temple's holy treasures were taken to Babylon. The Babylonians tore down the city walls. The line of Israelite kings (kings of Judah) descended from David now came to an end. The Israelites were no longer free or independent.

▷ The Ishtar Gate was one of eight gates into the inner city of Babylon. It was positioned on the processional way that led to the temple of Marduk, the main god of Babylon. Above ground the bricks were enameled and decorated. The gate was about 47ft high. When the Israelites were taken into exile there, Babylon was one of the wonders of the ancient world, a magnificent and wealthy city. Its many rivers and canals – some probably outside the city – are mentioned in Psalm 137: *"By the waters of Babylon . . . we sat down and wept."*

△ A bull decorating part of the foundations of the Ishtar Gate in Babylon. It is made of bricks specially shaped to give the animal's outline. These bricks, unlike those above ground level, were not coated with enamel.

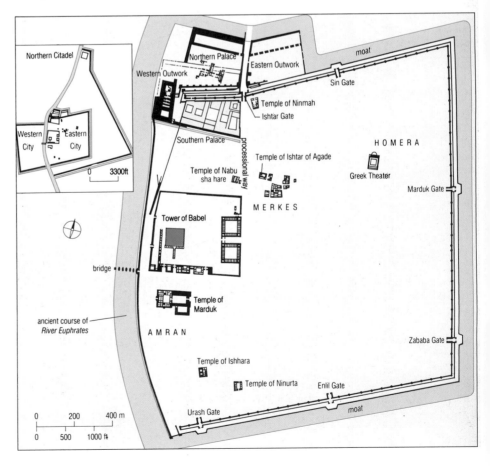

▷ Site plan of Babylon. As shown in the small plan, the river Euphrates divided the city – one of the "waters of Babylon" – into two parts. The larger plan shows the Ishtar Gate and the processional way. Ishtar was a goddess.

Babylon

CYRUS, RESTORER OF JUDAH

The Jews (as the Israelites are called from the 6th century BC) managed to survive the destruction of Jerusalem and their exile in Babylon. Two particular prophets helped them: Jeremiah, and the unknown prophet whose words are recorded in the book of Isaiah chapters 40 to 55.

Jeremiah

Jeremiah was active from about 626 to 585 BC. In his early preaching he had warned the Jews about a "foe from the north" that God would bring against Jerusalem. He repeated his warnings in about 605 BC – and a few years later the Babylonians captured and destroyed Jerusalem. The Jewish leaders called Jeremiah a traitor and imprisoned him. But his followers realized that his prophecy had come true – God had used the Babylonians to punish Jerusalem.

Predictions of the unnamed prophet

The Jewish exiles were dazzled by the mighty city and civilization of Babylon. Most of them believed that they had been defeated by a superior nation. But the prophet whose words

△ Tomb of Cyrus the Great at Pasargadae, modern Iran. The original inscription may have said: "*I am Cyrus who founded the Persian empire and was king of Asia.*"

◁ Cyrus conquered the former Assyrian and Babylonian empires, which in their time had ruled Israel and Judah. Under Cyrus' rule Jewish exiles returned to Jerusalem.

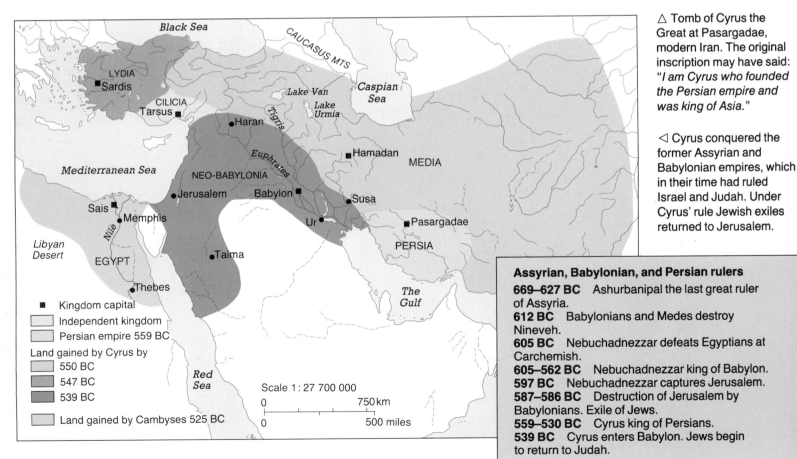

Kingdom capital
Independent kingdom
Persian empire 559 BC
Land gained by Cyrus by
550 BC
547 BC
539 BC
Land gained by Cambyses 525 BC

Scale 1 : 27 700 000
0   750 km
0   500 miles

Assyrian, Babylonian, and Persian rulers
669–627 BC Ashurbanipal the last great ruler of Assyria.
612 BC Babylonians and Medes destroy Nineveh.
605 BC Nebuchadnezzar defeats Egyptians at Carchemish.
605–562 BC Nebuchadnezzar king of Babylon.
597 BC Nebuchadnezzar captures Jerusalem.
587–586 BC Destruction of Jerusalem by Babylonians. Exile of Jews.
559–530 BC Cyrus king of Persians.
539 BC Cyrus enters Babylon. Jews begin to return to Judah.

◁ (inset) Part of a side door of one of the gates of Cyrus' tomb at Pasargadae, near Persepolis, in modern Iran. Cyrus died in 530 BC while campaigning with his armies in the east. The winged figure has an Egyptian-style headdress. Cyrus' name was carved into the stone in three languages.

△ The Cyrus Cylinder is in the British Museum, London. Part of the stone-carved message says: "*From . . . the cities . . . whose holy places had been in ruins . . . the gods who belong there I returned to their places . . . I gathered their inhabitants and restored to them their homes.*" This refers to the Jews' return to Jerusalem.

▽ Neco, king of Egypt, killed Josiah, king of Judah, at Megiddo when Josiah tried to stop him helping the Assyrians against the Babylonians. Babylon won and later invaded Judah and Egypt. Jews were taken as exiles to Babylon in 597, 587–6, and 582 BC. Other Jews fled to Egypt and settled there.

are in Isaiah chapters 40 to 55 had other views. The gods of the Babylonians were worthless objects of wood and gold, he said, carried around on carts. By contrast, Israel's God was real and powerful. He would free the Jews through the actions of Cyrus, king of Persia, who would defeat the Babylonians. In a striking passage in Isaiah chapter 45 verse 1, Cyrus is referred to as God's appointed servant.

Victories of King Cyrus

Cyrus became king of the Persians in 559 BC. In about 550 BC he defeated the Medes, who had helped the Babylonians conquer the Assyrians. He won some battles against the Babylonians in 539 BC before leading his army to the gates of Babylon; the city surrendered without a fight. Cyrus gave back the sacred images and objects that the Babylonians had taken from other peoples – including the Jews' temple treasures. He allowed the exiles to leave Babylon. So the Jews returned to Jerusalem, rebuilt the temple, and began worshiping there again. Cyrus recorded his action on a famous cylinder.

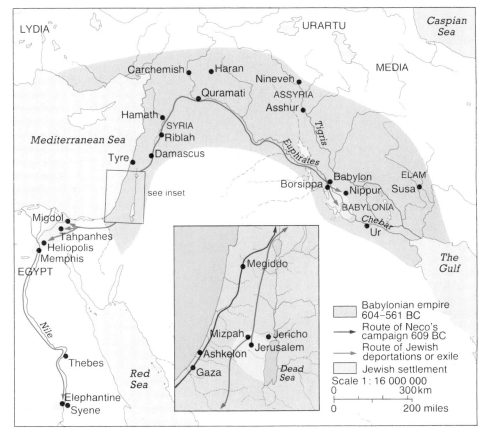

THE CONQUESTS OF ALEXANDER

The restored Jewish community in Judah was much smaller than the Jewish kingdom had been before 587 BC. Although the temple in Jerusalem was rebuilt, the walls of the city were still in ruins. Two men, Ezra and Nehemiah, who came from Persia in about 445 BC, did much to help the Jewish community recover and to rebuild Jerusalem.

Greeks and Persians

While the Jewish community struggled to re-establish itself in Judah at the beginning of the 5th century BC, the Persians tried to expand their empire. Their main opponents were the Greeks. Between 492 and 480 BC there were fierce battles between the Greeks and Persians. The Persians were defeated. One battle, fought at Marathon, has given its name to the famous long-distance race.

For the rest of the century and until about 360 BC, the Greeks fought among themselves. One Greek city-state, Sparta, tried unsuccessfully to invade Persia.

To the north of Greece was the kingdom of Macedon. In 359 BC Philip of Macedon began to enlarge his kingdom; by 338 BC he had conquered all of Greece. He did not live long enough to enjoy his victory; two years later he was murdered in his own court by a young man. Philip's son Alexander became king.

Alexander the Great

Alexander was only 20 when his father was murdered. Within 13 years he defeated Persia and Egypt and led his armies to the Indus river in India. He died in 323 BC aged only 33. After Alexander's second important victory against the Persians at Issus in 333 BC, he marched down through Syria to Egypt. The Jews became part of his Greek empire.

The Greek language began to spread into Syria and Egypt. So did Greek learning and culture, sport and the theater. New cities were built, modeled on the great cities of Greece. Within 100 years of Alexander's victory at Issus, many Jews lived in Egypt in the city named after him, Alexandria. Some of them began to translate the Bible from Hebrew into Greek. The fact that the New Testament was written in Greek shows how Alexander's conquests helped spread the Greek language.

◁ A marble sculpture of Alexander the Great, from a stone coffin (sarcophagus) in Turkey. Alexander was very famous in his lifetime, and many portrayals were made of him. Here he is shown as a noble fighter.

▷ Alexander's conquests. The map shows how Alexander crossed into Asia Minor and conquered the coast before turning inland and then to Issus. From there he led his troops through Syria into Egypt before returning to defeat the Persians one last time at Gaugamela. After that Alexander's armies marched east to India.

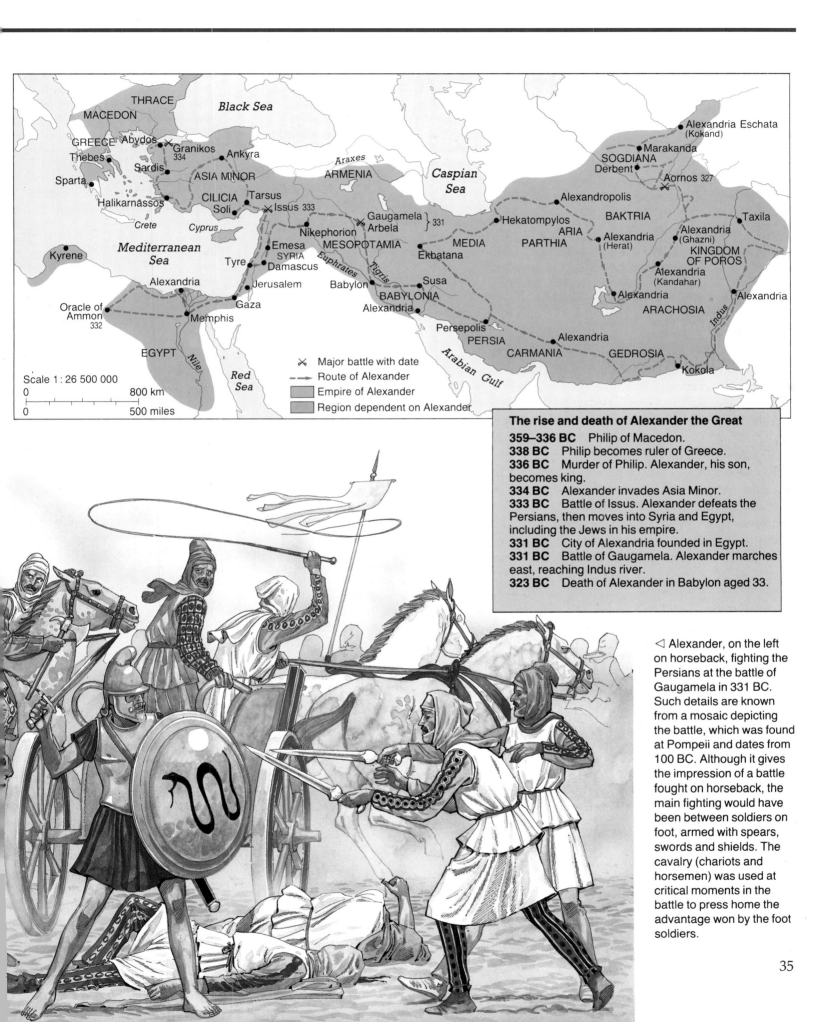

THRACE
MACEDON
Black Sea
GREECE Abydos ✕ Granikos
334 Ankyra
Thebes Sardis
Sparta ASIA MINOR
Halikarnassos CILICIA Tarsus
Soli ✕ Issus 333
Crete Cyprus
Araxes
ARMENIA
Caspian Sea
Alexandria Eschata (Kokand)
Marakanda
SOGDIANA
Derbent
Aornos 327 ✕
Alexandropolis
BAKTRIA
Taxila
ARIA
Alexandria (Herat)
PARTHIA
Alexandria (Ghazni)
KINGDOM OF POROS
Nikephorion
Gaugamela ✕ Arbela } 331
MESOPOTAMIA
Hekatompylos
MEDIA
Ekbatana
Alexandria (Kandahar)
Alexandria
Mediterranean Sea
Kyrene
Emesa SYRIA
Tyre Damascus
Euphrates Tigris
Babylon Susa
BABYLONIA
Alexandria
ARACHOSIA
Alexandria
Indus
Alexandria Jerusalem
Oracle of Ammon 332
Gaza Memphis
Persepolis
PERSIA
Alexandria
Alexandria
EGYPT
Nile
Red Sea
Arabian Gulf
CARMANIA
GEDROSIA
Kokola

Scale 1 : 26 500 000
0   800 km
0   500 miles

✕ Major battle with date
--→ Route of Alexander
▨ Empire of Alexander
▨ Region dependent on Alexander

The rise and death of Alexander the Great

359–336 BC   Philip of Macedon.
338 BC   Philip becomes ruler of Greece.
336 BC   Murder of Philip. Alexander, his son, becomes king.
334 BC   Alexander invades Asia Minor.
333 BC   Battle of Issus. Alexander defeats the Persians, then moves into Syria and Egypt, including the Jews in his empire.
331 BC   City of Alexandria founded in Egypt.
331 BC   Battle of Gaugamela. Alexander marches east, reaching Indus river.
323 BC   Death of Alexander in Babylon aged 33.

◁ Alexander, on the left on horseback, fighting the Persians at the battle of Gaugamela in 331 BC. Such details are known from a mosaic depicting the battle, which was found at Pompeii and dates from 100 BC. Although it gives the impression of a battle fought on horseback, the main fighting would have been between soldiers on foot, armed with spears, swords and shields. The cavalry (chariots and horsemen) was used at critical moments in the battle to press home the advantage won by the foot soldiers.

THE MACCABEAN REVOLT

After Alexander the Great died his empire was divided among his generals. Some of these men set themselves up as kings. From about 301 to 199 BC the Jews were under the control of Ptolemy, the king of Egypt, and his successors.

Antiochus III
Antiochus III was an ambitious king of northern Syria. By 199 BC he had taken control of Judah. At first Antiochus treated the Jews generously. But the struggle for Judah and competition for the right to collect taxes led to conflict between two powerful Jewish families: the Oniads, who controlled the high priesthood, and the Tobiads.

In 190 BC Antiochus was defeated by the Romans in Asia Minor. He lost land (but not Judah) and was forced to pay money to Rome. The next Syrian king, Seleucus IV, was so short of funds that he tried – without much success – to raid the Jews' temple treasury in Jerusalem.

Antiochus IV bans Judaism
Then Antiochus IV became king. He also badly needed money. Members of the Oniad and Tobiad families promised to help him in return for power. Jason, a Tobiad, bought the right to be high priest. He made part of Jerusalem into a Greek city, including a gymnasium

▷ A bronze representation of Zeus from the 5th century BC. Zeus was the chief of the gods of Mount Olympus, and many statues were made of him. The Maccabean revolt began when a statue in honor of Zeus was placed in the Jerusalem temple by Antiochus IV in 167 BC.

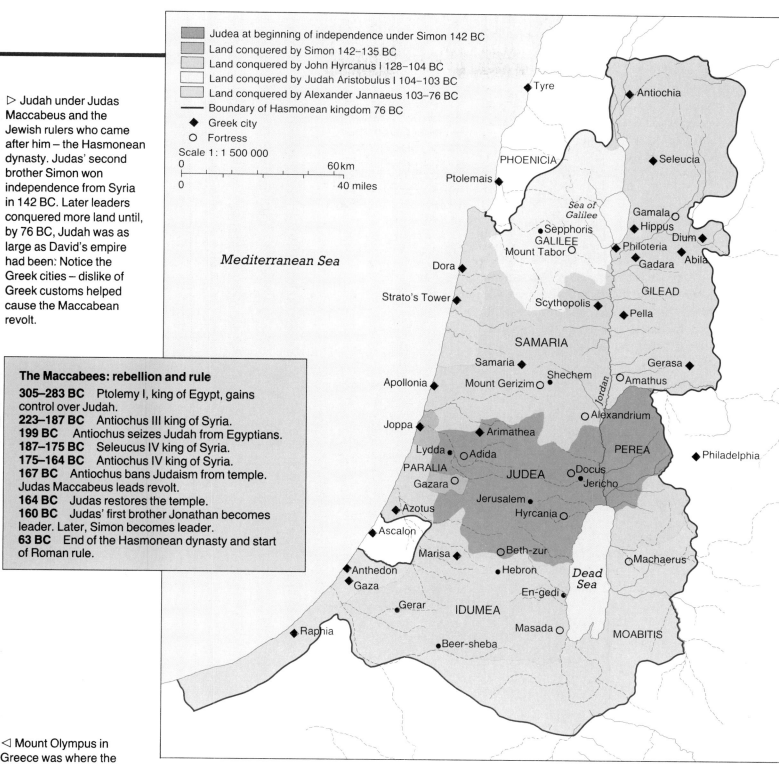

Judea at beginning of independence under Simon 142 BC
Land conquered by Simon 142–135 BC
Land conquered by John Hyrcanus I 128–104 BC
Land conquered by Judah Aristobulus I 104–103 BC
Land conquered by Alexander Jannaeus 103–76 BC
— Boundary of Hasmonean kingdom 76 BC
◆ Greek city
○ Fortress

Scale 1 : 1 500 000

0 ————————— 60km
0 ————————— 40 miles

Mediterranean Sea

PHOENICIA
Tyre ◆
Antiochia ◆
Ptolemais ◆
Seleucia ◆
Sea of Galilee
Gamala ○
Hippus ◆
Sepphoris ●
GALILEE
Mount Tabor ○
Philoteria ◆
Dium ◆
Gadara ◆
Abila
Dora ◆
GILEAD
Strato's Tower ◆
Scythopolis ◆
Pella ◆
SAMARIA
Samaria ◆
Gerasa ◆
Apollonia ◆
Shechem ●
Amathus ○
Mount Gerizim ○
Jordan
Joppa ◆
Alexandrium ○
Arimathea ◆
PEREA
Lydda ● ○ Adida
Philadelphia ◆
PARALIA
Docus ○
Gazara ○
JUDEA
Jericho ●
Jerusalem ●
Azotus ◆
Hyrcania ○
Ascalon
Beth-zur ○
Machaerus ○
Marisa ◆
Hebron ●
Dead Sea
Anthedon ◆
En-gedi ●
Gaza ◆
Gerar ●
IDUMEA
Masada ○
MOABITIS
Raphia ◆
Beer-sheba ●

▷ Judah under Judas Maccabeus and the Jewish rulers who came after him – the Hasmonean dynasty. Judas' second brother Simon won independence from Syria in 142 BC. Later leaders conquered more land until, by 76 BC, Judah was as large as David's empire had been: Notice the Greek cities – dislike of Greek customs helped cause the Maccabean revolt.

The Maccabees: rebellion and rule

305–283 BC Ptolemy I, king of Egypt, gains control over Judah.
223–187 BC Antiochus III king of Syria.
199 BC Antiochus seizes Judah from Egyptians.
187–175 BC Seleucus IV king of Syria.
175–164 BC Antiochus IV king of Syria.
167 BC Antiochus bans Judaism from temple. Judas Maccabeus leads revolt.
164 BC Judas restores the temple.
160 BC Judas' first brother Jonathan becomes leader. Later, Simon becomes leader.
63 BC End of the Hasmonean dynasty and start of Roman rule.

◁ Mount Olympus in Greece was where the Greeks believed that their gods met together. According to the ancient writer Hippias (400 BC), athletic games were held at Olympus from 776 BC. These sports, involving naked athletes, were popular with the Greeks. But when a gymnasium was built in Jerusalem in the 2nd century BC the Jews found this nakedness offensive.

where the athletes wore no clothes. To many Jews these actions were highly offensive.

Now that the person who promised the most money could become high priest, Jason was outbid by a man called Menelaus. The rivals began to fight each other. Antiochus restored order in Jerusalem, but used the occasion to plunder the temple. Because the Jews resisted his rule, in 167 BC Antiochus banned them from practicing their religion. A statue to the Greek god Zeus was set up in the temple.

Judas Maccabeus restores the temple

Jews loyal to their religion now rebelled against Antiochus, determined to recover their temple. Judas, nicknamed Maccabee or "hammer," led the revolt. The hilly country of Judah gave the rebels an advantage over the troops of Antiochus. Also, Antiochus had to fight other enemies elsewhere. In 164 BC Antiochus withdrew his ban on Israel's religion, and the temple was rededicated to God. Jews still celebrate this at the festival of Hanukkah.

HEROD THE GREAT

The southern part of Judah was called Idumea. Edomites – people from east of the river Jordan – had settled this land when the Jews went into exile in Babylon. Idumea had stayed non-Jewish until the Jewish king John Hyrcanus I (134/5–104 BC) had conquered it and converted the people to Judaism.

Herod becomes king

In the 1st century BC the Jewish kings came under the control of the Romans. Julius Caesar put an Idumean named Antipater in charge of Judea, as the Romans called Judah. His son, Herod, was appointed governor of Galilee. Some Jews felt that these Idumeans were not proper Jews.

Herod supported Mark Antony in the Roman civil wars and became king of Judea with his help. When Antony lost to Octavian a few years later, Herod kept his throne. He reigned until his death in 4 BC.

Rebuilding the temple

Herod began a great program of building throughout his land. The most important project was the rebuilding of the temple in Jerusalem; and some of the results can still be seen today. Herod enlarged the great platform on which the temple stood, making what was mainly a series of courtyards twice its former

▷ Aerial view of Machaerus, the Masada of the eastern side of the Jordan. It was first fortified by Alexander Jannaeus (103–76 BC) but rebuilt by Herod the Great as a huge fortress. According to the 1st-century AD Jewish historian Josephus, John the Baptist was imprisoned here by Herod Antipas.

▽ Herod's upper palace in Jerusalem was built on the summit of the western hill overlooking the temple area. At the northeastern end (left in the picture) were three towers, of which two are visible here. In front of them can be seen a large central garden with a pool in the middle. During the time of Jesus the Roman governors of Judea used the palace as their residence in Jerusalem. It was probably here that Pontius Pilate tried Jesus.

size. The work continued long after his death and was finished only a few years before the temple was destroyed by the Romans in AD 70.

Herod's palaces, and Caesarea

Herod had a number of palaces built for himself, remains of which have survived. These were constructed in the Greco-Roman style,

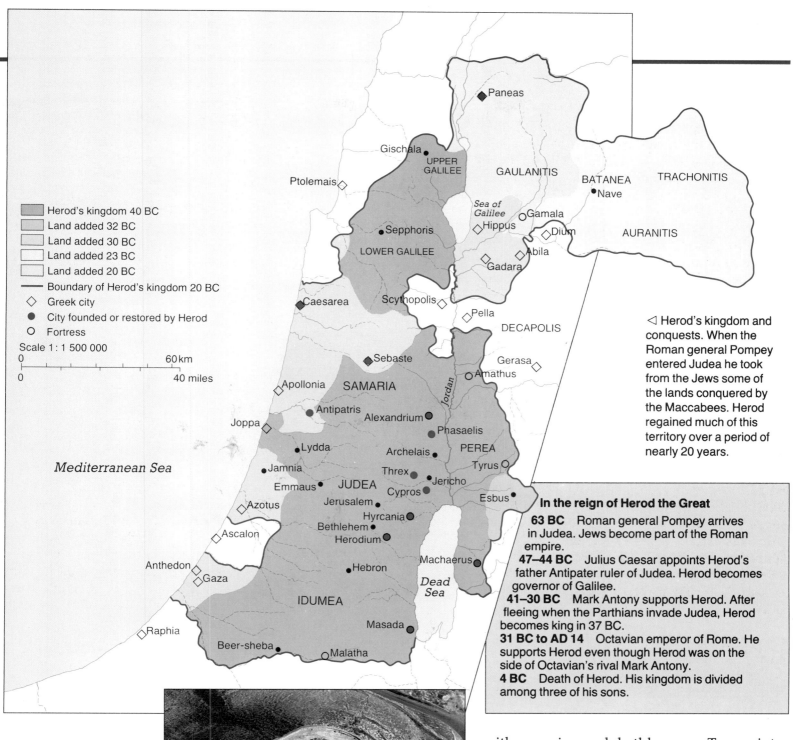

Herod's kingdom 40 BC
Land added 32 BC
Land added 30 BC
Land added 23 BC
Land added 20 BC
Boundary of Herod's kingdom 20 BC
◇ Greek city
● City founded or restored by Herod
○ Fortress

Scale 1 : 1 500 000
0 ———————— 60 km
0 ———————— 40 miles

Mediterranean Sea

Paneas

Gischala
UPPER GALILEE
GAULANITIS
BATANEA
Nave
TRACHONITIS

Ptolemais ◇

Sea of Galilee
Gamala
Hippus ◇
Dium ◇
AURANITIS

Sepphoris
LOWER GALILEE
Abila ◇
Gadara ◇

Caesarea ◆
Scythopolis ◇
Pella ◇
DECAPOLIS

Sebaste ◆
Gerasa ◇

Apollonia ◇
SAMARIA
Amathus ○

Antipatris ●
Alexandrium ○

Joppa ◇
Phasaelis ●

Lydda ●
Archelais ●
PEREA

Jamnia ●
Threx ○
Tyrus ○

Emmaus ●
JUDEA
Cypros ○
Jericho ●

Azotus ◇
Jerusalem ●
Esbus ●

Hyrcania ○
Bethlehem ●
Ascalon ◇
Herodium ●

Machaerus ○

Anthedon ◇
Hebron ●
Dead Sea

Gaza ◇
IDUMEA

Raphia ◇
Masada ○

Beer-sheba ●
Malatha ○

Jordan

◁ Herod's kingdom and conquests. When the Roman general Pompey entered Judea he took from the Jews some of the lands conquered by the Maccabees. Herod regained much of this territory over a period of nearly 20 years.

In the reign of Herod the Great

63 BC   Roman general Pompey arrives in Judea. Jews become part of the Roman empire.
47–44 BC   Julius Caesar appoints Herod's father Antipater ruler of Judea. Herod becomes governor of Galilee.
41–30 BC   Mark Antony supports Herod. After fleeing when the Parthians invade Judea, Herod becomes king in 37 BC.
31 BC to AD 14   Octavian emperor of Rome. He supports Herod even though Herod was on the side of Octavian's rival Mark Antony.
4 BC   Death of Herod. His kingdom is divided among three of his sons.

▷ Herodium, Herod's summer palace in the Judean Hills 7½ miles south of Jerusalem. This impressive man-made hill can be seen from Jerusalem. Remains of the four towers are visible at the corners. Herod may have been buried in the north tower. At the foot of the mound was a large town where many people lived. Excavation of the site is just beginning.

with mosaics and bathhouses. Two winter palaces were built in the Jordan valley, which stays warm in the winter; one of these was at Jericho, the other at Masada by the Dead Sea. Herod had a summer palace built at Herodium, to the south of Bethlehem, where it was cool in the summer. The site is easily recognizable today by its unusual cone shape.

Another large building project of Herod's was at Caesarea on the Mediterranean coast. This provided the kingdom with a great harbor and storehouses. To bring water to the city magnificent aqueducts were constructed – their remains are still a splendid sight.

JESUS' HIDDEN YEARS

Jesus first came to public notice in about AD 28 when he began to preach and to heal the sick in Galilee. His life ended less than three years later when the Romans nailed him to a cross in Jerusalem.

Dating the birth of Jesus

Matthew's Gospel (chapter 2 verse 1) tells us that Jesus was born during Herod's reign. So Jesus was born before 4 BC, probably about 6 BC. It may seem strange that Jesus Christ was born six years "before Christ." But the scholars who invented our BC/AD dating system in the 17th century made mistakes because they knew less than we do today about past history.

Bethlehem and Nazareth

When Jesus began to preach and heal in Galilee his place of birth was a mystery to most people. Only after the Gospels of Matthew and Luke were written was it widely known that he had been born in Bethlehem.

Why was Jesus born in Bethlehem? Luke (chapter 2 verse 1) says that Jesus' parents went to Bethlehem because a census had been ordered and Joseph came from Bethlehem. Matthew (chapter 2 verse 11) says that the wise men from the East visited the family of Jesus in a *house* in Bethlehem; he suggests that Jesus' family moved from Bethlehem to Nazareth after Herod's death.

Jesus' boyhood

Nazareth, where Jesus grew up, was such a small place that you will not find it on our maps about the Maccabees and Herod the Great. The nearest important town was Sepphoris.

According to Mark's Gospel (chapter 6 verse 3), Jesus was a carpenter. Because his father is not mentioned in this passage, it is possible that Joseph had died when Jesus was a boy. The Gospel tells of four brothers and a number of sisters. As the eldest, Jesus would probably have taken responsibility for maintaining the family after his father's death.

The only story told about Jesus' boyhood was the visit to Jerusalem described by Luke (chapter 2 verses 41 to 52). Jesus, then aged 12, stayed on after his parents had left for home. They returned to find him in the temple talking with learned teachers.

◁ The 6th-century AD church of the Nativity in Bethlehem. It is built over the cave that has been considered the place of Jesus' birth since the 2nd century AD. The animals of the inn were kept in a cave, not in a shed.

▽ Bethlehem is a small town in the Judean Hills. To the east (behind the buildings in the photo) begins the Judean Desert. Today the town has many Christian churches.

Walls of Justinian

grotto of the Nativity

St Jerome's cell

St Jerome's cenotaph

sepulcher

Constantinian walls

0   10m

0   30ft

△ The carpenter was one of the most important people in a small town in Jesus' time. Wood was the main material for making tools such as plows and yokes, which attached plows to animals. (Iron was used only for such items as the tip of the plow or head of an axe or hoe, as seen here.) Household furniture was also made from wood. Both Jesus and his father Joseph are called carpenters in the Bible, and Jesus would have been his father's apprentice until he had learned the trade for himself. When he began his ministry, Jesus thought of his first followers rather as apprentices, called to learn how to work in the service of God.

▷ Nazareth is in lower Galilee. In Jesus' time it was just a village. Today it is dominated by the church of the Annunciation, a building that was completed in the 1960s. The Annunciation was the event described in the Gospel of Luke when an angel announced to Mary that she would give birth to Jesus.

JESUS' MINISTRY IN GALILEE

In about AD 27 a man known as John the Baptist began to preach. He said that the time was close when God would bring judgment to the Jewish people by means of a person mightier than John himself. People came from all parts of the land to the river Jordan. There John baptized them as a sign that they wished God to forgive the wrong things they had done.

The beginning of Jesus' ministry

Among those who came to be baptized was Jesus. When John saw Jesus he recognized him as the one whose coming he had announced. He felt unworthy of baptizing Jesus, but Jesus insisted.

During his baptism Jesus heard the voice of God calling him to special work. He afterward spent a period of quiet alone in the wilderness, going without food; this was when he decided how he would do God's work.

Most of Jesus' public preaching and healing of the sick took place in Galilee. He began to gather a group of followers there, called disciples. Some of them were fishermen. Jesus lodged in the house of Peter, one of his disciples, in Capernaum – a town on the northern shore of the Sea of Galilee.

What Jesus taught

Jesus taught that God was at work in new ways in the world. God would help people to be better men and women and help them live

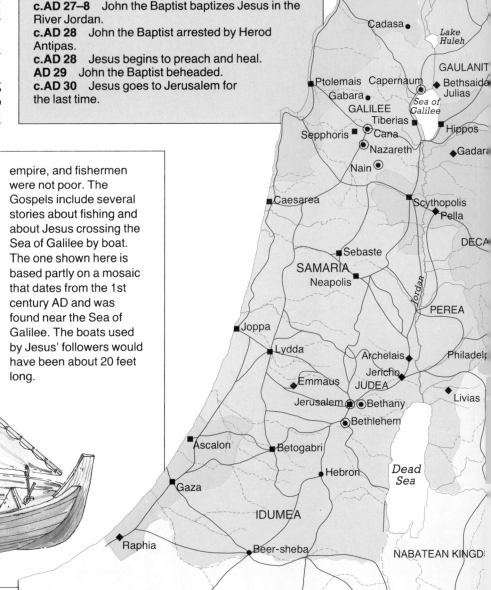

▽ The main places in Jesus' ministry. Jesus made Capernaum his base and did most of his work in Galilee, often teaching beside the Sea of Galilee. As far as we know, he did not preach in such cities as Tiberias or Sepphoris.

Life and times of Jesus and John the Baptist

AD 14–37 Tiberius emperor of Rome.
AD 26–36 Pontius Pilate is Roman governor of Judea.
c.AD 27 Ministry of John the Baptist near River Jordan.
c.AD 27–8 John the Baptist baptizes Jesus in the River Jordan.
c.AD 28 John the Baptist arrested by Herod Antipas.
c.AD 28 Jesus begins to preach and heal.
AD 29 John the Baptist beheaded.
c.AD 30 Jesus goes to Jerusalem for the last time.

▽ The first followers of Jesus were fishermen. The Sea of Galilee contained fish that were sold in the Roman empire, and fishermen were not poor. The Gospels include several stories about fishing and about Jesus crossing the Sea of Galilee by boat. The one shown here is based partly on a mosaic that dates from the 1st century AD and was found near the Sea of Galilee. The boats used by Jesus' followers would have been about 20 feet long.

Chronology of the Life of Jesus
Note: this is based mainly on Mark's Gospel which assumes that Jesus went only once to Jerusalem during his public ministry. John's Gospel tells us that Jesus visited Jerusalem several times during this period.

c. 6 BC   Birth of Jesus.
c. AD 7   Jesus visits Jerusalem with his parents and is left behind. He is found in the temple discussing with learned teachers.
c. 27   Beginning of ministry of John the Baptist.
c. 28   Jesus is baptized by John and withdraws to the Judean Desert to fast and pray. Later he begins his public ministry in Galilee.
c. 29   Execution of John the Baptist. Jesus withdraws from Galilee to the territory ruled by Herod's son Philip. At Caesarea Philippi he asks his disciples who they think he is, and Peter declares that Jesus is the Messiah.
c. 30   Jesus begins to travel to Jerusalem. His route takes him through Galilee, along the Jordan valley, through Jericho and up to Bethany. From here he makes his triumphal entry to Jerusalem. On the evening of 14 Nisan (7 April) he eats the Last Supper with his followers, and that night is arrested, tried, and condemned to death. On the afternoon of 14 Nisan (the day is reckoned to start the previous evening) Jesus is crucified. On the morning of 16 Nisan his body is missing from the tomb and his followers believe that God has raised him from death.

together in love and peace. Jesus' own followers were an example of this. They came from different backgrounds and would not normally have mixed; they also included women, which was unusual at the time. Some people were amazed at how Jesus accepted them, and how this changed their lives.

Jesus said harsh things against the religious people who would not listen to him. For ordinary, uneducated people Jesus put his teaching in the form of simple stories called parables. The crowds flocked to hear him.

Did Jesus fail in Galilee?
In a way, Jesus' work in Galilee failed. Some people wanted him only so that he would heal their illnesses. Religious leaders rejected him because he was an outsider. Others were more interested in overthrowing Roman rule.

Even Jesus' closest friends did not fully understand him. They could not believe his teaching that the greatest person is the one who is the servant of others.

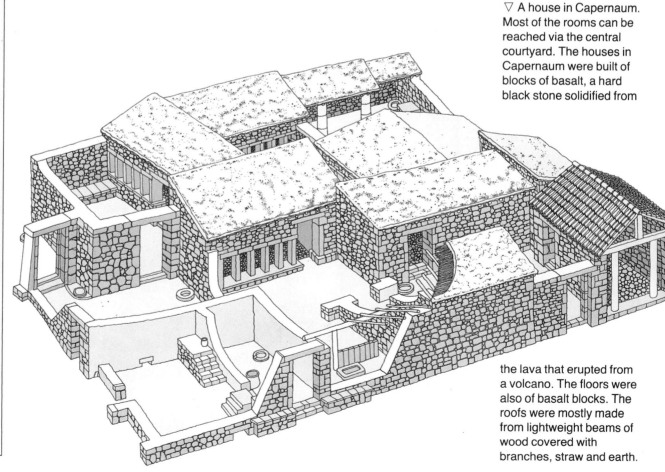

▽ A house in Capernaum. Most of the rooms can be reached via the central courtyard. The houses in Capernaum were built of blocks of basalt, a hard black stone solidified from the lava that erupted from a volcano. The floors were also of basalt blocks. The roofs were mostly made from lightweight beams of wood covered with branches, straw and earth.

HEROD'S TEMPLE IN JERUSALEM

Herod's temple in Jerusalem was the third built on the site. The first temple had been completed by Solomon in about 950 BC. This was more of a royal chapel than a place of public worship. When Josiah reformed the practice of Israel's religion in 622 BC Jerusalem became a holy place for all the Jewish nation. After the Babylonians destroyed Solomon's temple a second temple was built by Zerubbabel in 515 BC. This was less grand than Solomon's temple – and Herod rebuilt much of it.

Size and layout of Herod's temple

Herod extended a great platform for his temple. It was roughly a rectangle, its longer sides about 500 yards and the shorter sides about 300 yards long. The most important part of the building, which only Jews could enter, was therefore set in a great courtyard.

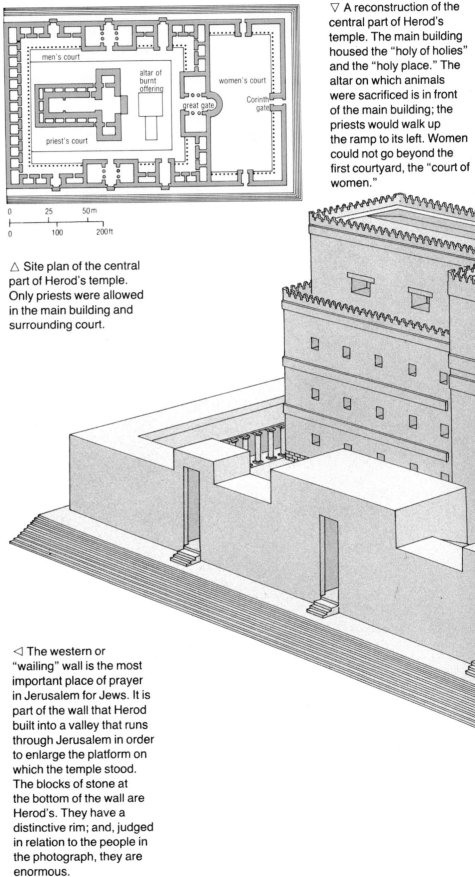

△ Site plan of the central part of Herod's temple. Only priests were allowed in the main building and surrounding court.

▽ A reconstruction of the central part of Herod's temple. The main building housed the "holy of holies" and the "holy place." The altar on which animals were sacrificed is in front of the main building; the priests would walk up the ramp to its left. Women could not go beyond the first courtyard, the "court of women."

◁ The western or "wailing" wall is the most important place of prayer in Jerusalem for Jews. It is part of the wall that Herod built into a valley that runs through Jerusalem in order to enlarge the platform on which the temple stood. The blocks of stone at the bottom of the wall are Herod's. They have a distinctive rim; and, judged in relation to the people in the photograph, they are enormous.

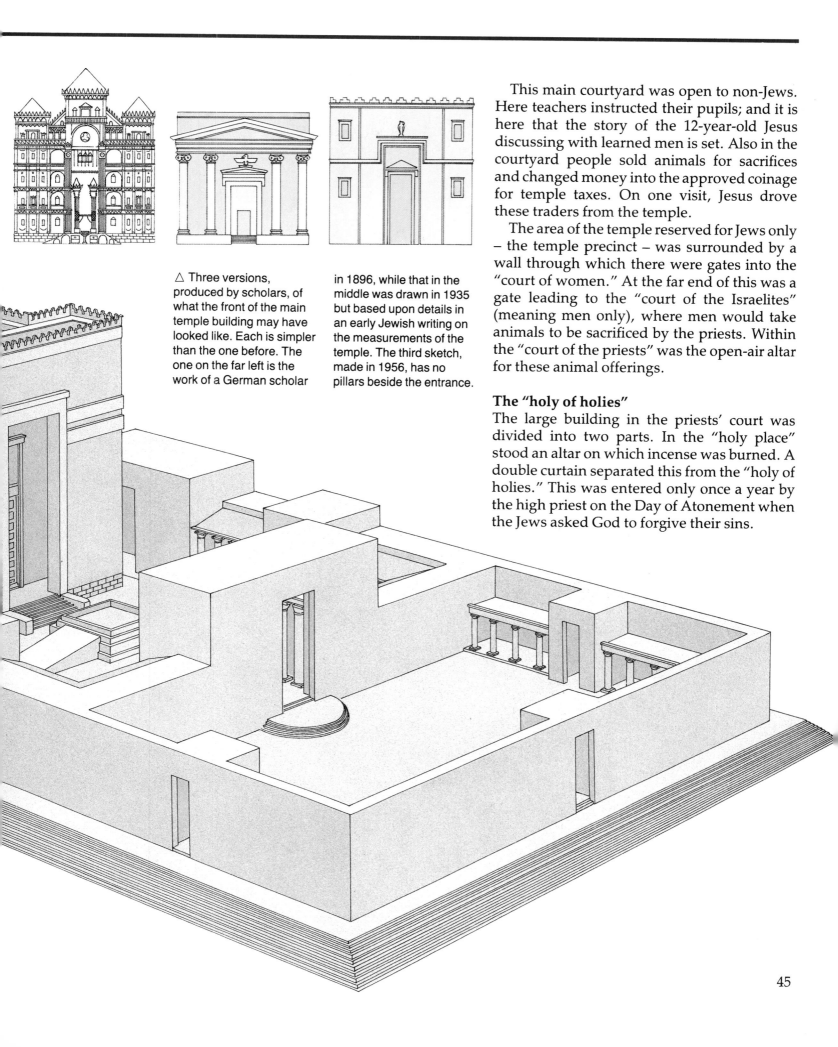

△ Three versions, produced by scholars, of what the front of the main temple building may have looked like. Each is simpler than the one before. The one on the far left is the work of a German scholar in 1896, while that in the middle was drawn in 1935 but based upon details in an early Jewish writing on the measurements of the temple. The third sketch, made in 1956, has no pillars beside the entrance.

This main courtyard was open to non-Jews. Here teachers instructed their pupils; and it is here that the story of the 12-year-old Jesus discussing with learned men is set. Also in the courtyard people sold animals for sacrifices and changed money into the approved coinage for temple taxes. On one visit, Jesus drove these traders from the temple.

The area of the temple reserved for Jews only – the temple precinct – was surrounded by a wall through which there were gates into the "court of women." At the far end of this was a gate leading to the "court of the Israelites" (meaning men only), where men would take animals to be sacrificed by the priests. Within the "court of the priests" was the open-air altar for these animal offerings.

The "holy of holies"

The large building in the priests' court was divided into two parts. In the "holy place" stood an altar on which incense was burned. A double curtain separated this from the "holy of holies." This was entered only once a year by the high priest on the Day of Atonement when the Jews asked God to forgive their sins.

THE PASSION OF JESUS

Crucifixion was a Roman form of execution reserved for common criminals and foreigners. Although the Romans crucified hundreds of Jews, only one body of a crucified man has ever been found. His arms had been tied to the crosspiece by rope. His legs were nailed to the upright. In the case of Jesus, it is believed his arms and his legs were nailed to the cross.

Crucifixion meant a slow and painful death, yet Jesus willingly accepted death in order to show that God's love is stronger than human wickedness. His suffering and death on the cross are known as his Passion.

Entry into Jerusalem
Jesus set out from Galilee to celebrate the Passover in Jerusalem with his disciples in about AD 30. As he came in sight of the city he mounted a donkey, riding into Jerusalem to the cheers of the crowds. People greeted Jesus as a king coming in peace. His first act was to go to the temple and to drive out the money-changers and traders from what was supposed to be a place of prayer.

The Last Supper
On the last evening of his life Jesus ate the Passover meal with his 12 closest followers. He spoke of his own sacrifice to come. At his disciples' future meals, Jesus said, bread and wine would represent his body, which was about to be killed, and his blood, which would soon be shed.

Arrest, trial, and execution
The religious leaders wanted to have Jesus executed by the Romans because, they said, he claimed to be a king. After the Last Supper he was arrested in the Garden of Gethsemane. A religious council called the Sanhedrin put him on trial and handed him over to the Roman governor Pontius Pilate. Pilate was not convinced that Jesus should be put to death, but he allowed the execution.

Helped by a passer-by, Jesus carried the crosspiece of his cross to the place of crucifixion outside the city. The crowds who had cheered him before mocked him now along the way. His disciples deserted him. Only a small group of women, including his mother, stayed with Jesus to the end.

◁ Steps possibly dating from New Testament times close to where the house of the high priest may have stood, now in the grounds of the church of St Peter in Gallicantu. Jesus was taken to the house after his arrest. It was here that Peter denied knowing Jesus. The way from the Garden of Gethsemane to the house was via flights of steps up from the valley at the foot of the western hill.

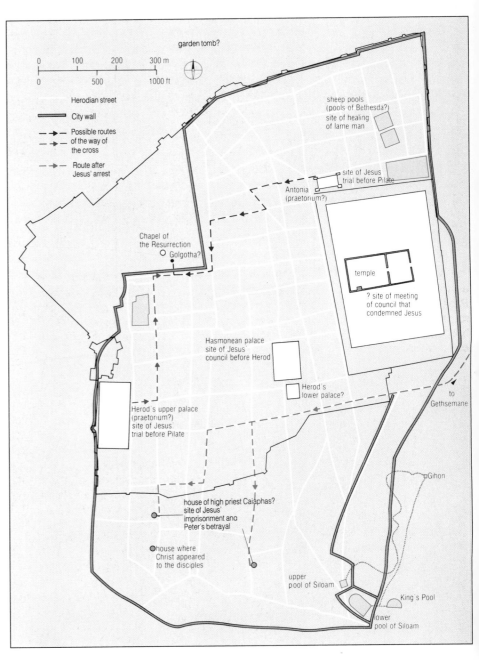

garden tomb?

0   100   200   300 m
0   500   1000 ft

Herodian street

City wall

Possible routes of the way of the cross

Route after Jesus' arrest

sheep pools (pools of Bethesda?) site of healing of lame man

site of Jesus' trial before Pilate

Antonia (praetorium?)

Chapel of the Resurrection
O Golgotha?

temple

? site of meeting of council that condemned Jesus

Hasmonean palace site of Jesus' council before Herod

Herod's lower palace?

to Gethsemane

Herod's upper palace (praetorium?) site of Jesus' trial before Pilate

Gihon

house of high priest Caiaphas? site of Jesus' imprisonment and Peter's betrayal

house where Christ appeared to the disciples

upper pool of Siloam

King's Pool

lower pool of Siloam

◁ Places and routes associated with the Passion of Jesus. Both the route to the high priest's house and the way of the cross are shown.

▽ After his death Jesus' body was laid in a tomb similar to the one shown here. The round stone used to close the tomb can be clearly seen.

△ This painting of the Deposition (after his Crucifixion) by Rogier van der Weyden (c. 1400–64) captures the grief of the mourners.

▷ The site usually considered to be where the Garden of Gethsemane was, where Jesus was arrested. The ancient olive trees in the picture may be 1,000 years old. The name of the garden indicates that there was a press there for making oil. Today the Church of All Nations stands in part of the garden.

47

PAUL AND THE SPREAD OF CHRISTIANITY

When several weeks had passed after the death of Jesus, his followers began to preach in public. They said that he had risen from death and was God's anointed servant, as promised in the Old Testament.

Nobody could produce the body of Jesus to disprove them. And if Jesus' disciples had stolen the body, why would they lie and risk being imprisoned or put to death? The number of believers grew quickly, but so did the strength of feeling against them.

Paul's conversion

The first believer to lose his life for his faith in Jesus was Stephen. A young man named Saul was among the people who saw him stoned to death. Saul's Greek name was Paul. He came from Tarsus in Asia Minor. He was a devout Jew and, unusually, also a Roman citizen.

Paul was at first one of those who disliked the believers in Jesus, and he helped others arrest and imprison them. Then, however, on a journey to Damascus after witnessing Stephen's death, he had a vision of Jesus. This changed him into a believer.

The church at Antioch

The city of Antioch, on the coast of northern Syria, was the place where the followers of Jesus were first called Christians. From here they set out to take Christianity into the Roman empire. Paul became a member of the church at Antioch, and he made three great journeys from the city between AD 46 and AD 57.

Paul always preached first to groups of Jews when he came to a new city. But non-Jews also accepted his message. Some Christians believed that non-Jews who became Christians should keep the Jewish law as given by God to Moses. Paul disagreed.

Paul's arrest and trials

Some Jews hated Paul, who believed that Jewish law was not binding on non-Jews who became Christians. Visiting Jerusalem in AD 58 he was almost killed by a mob. He was imprisoned and sent to Caesarea, where he spent two years pleading his innocence. He appealed to Rome for justice and in about AD 59 sailed to Rome, surviving a shipwreck. He is said to have been executed a few years later.

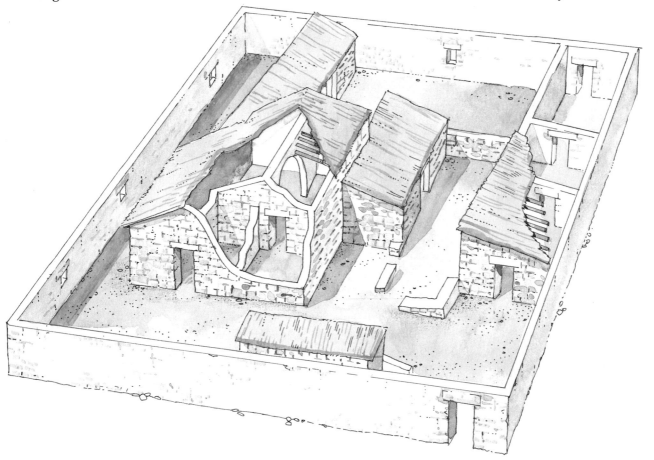

▷ Paul's journeys. Beginning from Antioch, Paul went first to Cyprus and Asia Minor before returning to the Syrian city. The second and third journeys included Greece and Jerusalem. On his final journey he was shipwrecked at Malta before eventually reaching Rome.

◁ An artist's impression of one of the early places of Christian worship in the eastern Mediterranean region. The first believers in Jesus gathered in houses such as that of Peter in Capernaum. Those who met there wrote prayers or Christian verses on the walls. Here, the cut-away roof enables us to see how two inner rooms have been joined into one to make a bigger space for the worshippers to gather. As time went on, the room for worship was made bigger, and eventually it became a church.

◁ A mosaic of Paul from the crypt (underground room) of St Peter's in Rome. A description of Paul in The Acts of Paul and Thecla, a 2nd-century AD text, says that he was small, bald, and bowlegged. He may also have been short-sighted. However, Paul did more than anyone in the 1st century AD to ensure the spread of Christianity.

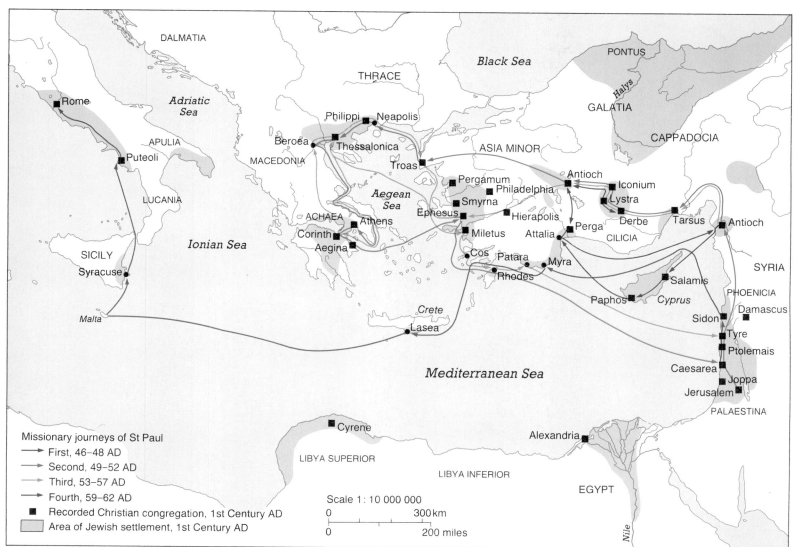

Missionary journeys of St Paul
→ First, 46–48 AD
→ Second, 49–52 AD
→ Third, 53–57 AD
→ Fourth, 59–62 AD
■ Recorded Christian congregation, 1st Century AD
  Area of Jewish settlement, 1st Century AD

Scale 1 : 10 000 000

0   300km

0   200 miles

PART TWO

THE GEOGRAPHY OF THE BIBLE LANDS

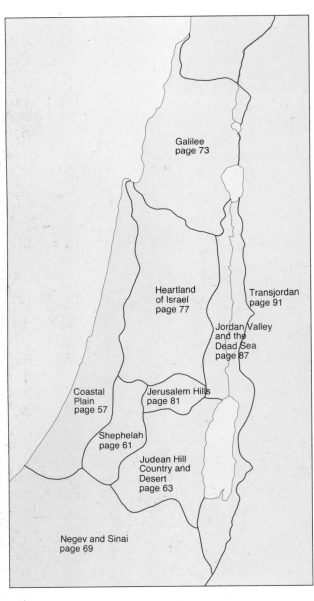

▷ This Jewish place of worship (synagogue) in Capernaum dates from the 4th or 5th century AD. It stands on the site of a synagogue where Jesus preached.

THE GEOGRAPHY OF THE HOLY LAND

The land of the Bible is full of contrasts. Each region has its own landscape. There are striking differences in height – and variations in temperature and climate too.

The coastal plain and the Shephelah
The coastal plain is the strip of land next to the Mediterranean Sea. It begins just above the town of Nahariyya in the north and follows the coastline southward to Mount Carmel. The plain then continues and widens southward. Finally it merges into the Negev Desert and Sinai. Shephelah is Hebrew for "lowlands." This beautiful area of broad valleys and rolling hills links the coastal plain and the Judean and Jerusalem Hills.

Judean Hills and Desert, the Negev and Sinai
The Judean Hills are at the southern end of the central uplands that stretch south from Galilee. Bordered by the Jerusalem Hills to the north, the Shephelah to the west, and the Negev to the south, to the east they run down through the Judean Desert to the Dead Sea. The desert here is not a wilderness of sand; grass grows and sheep graze in winter.

The Negev is the dry area to the south of the Judean Hills, bordered by the modern frontier with Egypt. South and west of the Negev is the larger and often mountainous Sinai Desert.

Galilee and the Jerusalem Hills
Upper Galilee includes the Meron Mountains, some of which are over 3,280 ft high. There are no easy routes over these uplands. Coming south into lower Galilee, the hills get gentler. Farther south still, the broad, triangle-shaped plain, known in the Bible as the valley of Jezreel, runs from the coastal plain at Mount Carmel to the Jordan valley.

The land to the south climbs toward the Samaria Hills. A ridge of uplands stretches southward to Jerusalem, Hebron, and beyond. Between Ramallah and Jerusalem is the saddle of lower, flatter land known as the Jerusalem Hills.

The Jordan valley and Transjordan
The river Jordan is fed by springs from the snow on Mount Hermon. The Jordan flows south into the Sea of Galilee, whose surface is 690 ft *below* sea level; and as the river continues south to the Dead Sea the valley gets even lower. The surface of the Dead Sea is 1,310 ft below sea level. Its shores are the lowest land on earth.

Transjordan is the hilly land east of the river Jordan. Spectacular gorges (deep and narrow valleys) cut through these hills. From here the Syrian Desert stretches away to the east.

△ This spectacular picture shows one of the strange landscapes found in Israel. Here, in the wilderness of the Negev Desert large rounded rocks have been formed by wind and rain over thousands of years.

▷ The present-day land of the Bible. Central hills stretch north–south and the rivers run east–west. The hills reach the coastal plain at Mount Carmel.

▽ A cross-section of the southern part of the Holy Land shows the variations in height. The Judean Hills go down in "steps" to the Jordan valley.

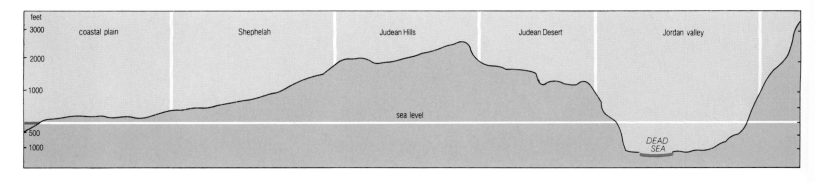

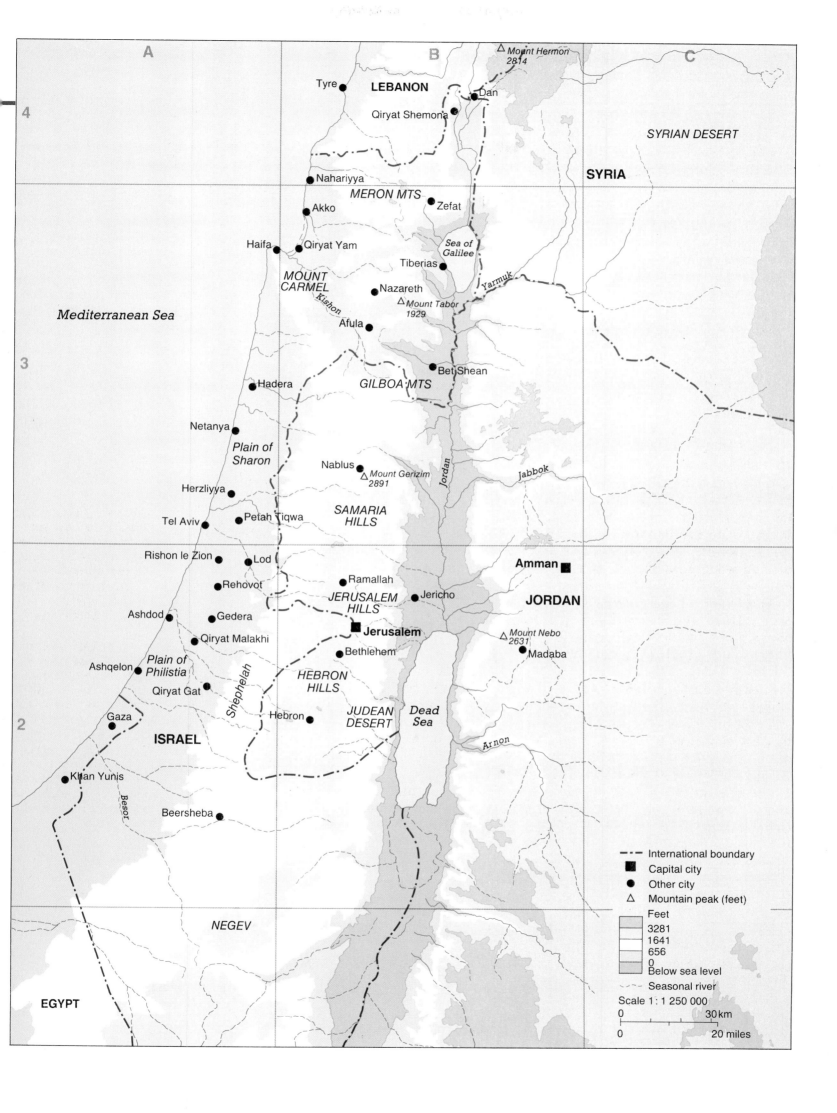

THE LANDSCAPE OF THE BIBLE

If you visit the Holy Land today you will see a landscape that has changed greatly since the time of the Bible. The same would be true if you were studying what parts of Europe looked like 2,000 or more years ago.

Once a land of forests

One major difference between the Holy Land in biblical times and now is the presence today of large cities such as Tel Aviv and Jerusalem, motorways, and airports. But not everywhere is more heavily populated now than then. In New Testament times more people lived around the Sea of Galilee, for example, than live there today.

Another important change is the lack of trees today. Like many other parts of the world, the land of the Bible has lost the great forests that once covered it. In the case of ancient Israel, this loss was especially serious.

We have seen that the land is very hilly; and when it rains there, the rainfall is very heavy. Most of the forests in the Holy Land were of evergreen oaks that did not change their leaves until the rains were over in April. The leaves broke the force of the heavy rains, so that the water did not damage the soil.

Over the centuries the forests were cut down – for building materials and firewood and to clear land for farming. The rains began to wash the soils down into the valleys. In some places this left a badly eroded landscape, such as that shown opposite.

Seasons and climate

The Holy Land had two main seasons – as there still are in this part of the world. The cool, wet period lasted from October to April, and the warm, dry period from May to September. The time for growing crops was the winter. Although it can become cold, the ground temperature is warm enough for plants to grow; and this is the only time of year when it rains. In the summer it was too dry for crops or flowers to flourish.

In the Bible the word "famine" occurs over a hundred times. The rain often did not come. This meant that food crops could not be sown, because the ground was rock hard after the dry summer. Rainfall was highest in Galilee, and lower on the hills of Judea.

The agricultural year

In September and October, Israelite villagers would gather olives from the olive trees and press them for oil. If the rain came in October, they could plow the land and sow barley and wheat, lentils, and chickpeas. Between February and March they cut grasses and weeds to use as hay for their animals. Barley was harvested in April, wheat in May. The final summer tasks were the gathering of grapes, figs, and dates from July to September.

▷ This vegetation map of ancient Israel shows clearly how much forest there was. The main areas of farmland shown were mainly for cereal crops (barley and wheat) and fruit (dates, olives, figs, grapes, pomegranates). Flax was also grown, for linenmaking. Small pockets of land were used throughout the land area for grazing cattle, goats, and sheep. Large parts of the coastal plain were too marshy or sandy for farming.

▷ It is hard to believe that this landscape, not far from Jerusalem, was once covered by evergreen oak trees. The destruction of the forests began after 4000 BC. But in Old Testament times there were still enough of them for the lions and bears they sheltered to be a danger to people.

Vegetation of ancient Israel
- Oasis
- Farmland
- Marsh
- Mixed dwarf shrub
- Grassland and shrubs
- Forest and maquis
- Sand dunes
- Semi-desert
- Desert

Tyre
Lake Huleh
Hazo
Acco
Sea of Galilee
Megiddo
Beth-shean
Mediterranean Sea
Shechem
Jordan
Aphek
Joppa
Jericho
Ashdod
Jerusalem
Ashkelon
Gaza
Hebron
Dead Sea
Beer-sheba

Scale 1 : 1 500 000
0   20 km
0   20 miles

THE SOUTHERN COASTAL PLAIN

Of all the main parts of the land of the Bible, no section has changed more than the southern coastal plain. This plain runs from Mount Carmel in the north down to the Negev coast, near Gaza, in the south. In biblical times only small numbers of people lived here beside the Mediterranean Sea; but today it is the most heavily populated area of Israel.

Coastline ridges, marshes, and dunes

During the millions of years that the Earth as we know it was being formed, the sea came in and went out three times along the Mediterranean coast of Israel. Each time the sea advanced, it formed a coastline of hard rocks. So there have been three coastlines in all – the present one, and two more inland, which today are ridges of hard rock.

These ridges blocked the flow of the rivers that carried rainwater and springwater westward to the Mediterranean Sea. As a result, marshes formed. Nearest to the sea there were sand dunes. In those large parts of the coastal plain that consisted of dunes and marshes, it was not easy to live or to travel.

△ The stone head of a man in Greek style found at Dor, one of the few places where it was possible to have a seaport on the Mediterranean. Dor became Israelite during the reign of David. It gave its name to an Assyrian district in the 8th century BC.

From forests to farming

For a distance of nearly 20 mi south from Mount Carmel the plain is less than 2 mi wide; but as you travel farther south it becomes as wide as 10 mi. Forests of oak and pine once stood in some parts of the plain. The last of these remained until nearly 80 years ago, when they were cut down by the Turkish rulers of the land to provide fuel for the railways.

Nowadays the plain is an important farming region, producing fruit and vegetables.

People of the coastal plain

In Old Testament times the southern coastal plain was where the Philistines settled in the 12th century BC. Their towns were near the Shephelah to the southeast where it joins the plain. The struggles between the Israelite hero Samson and the Philistines took place here. The blinded Samson died at Gaza.

The most important route from Egypt northward also followed the plain, hugging the hills to the east. It was known as the Way of the Sea. Today the plain contains the Israeli city of Tel Aviv, with over a million inhabitants.

◁ Marshlands on the coastal plain. Even today the ridges formed by Israel's ancient coastlines can stop rainwater and springwater reaching the Mediterranean. At the bottom of the picture is today's coastline of sandy cliffs edged with dunes. In the distance are the lower hills of the Shephelah, backed by the higher Judean Hills.

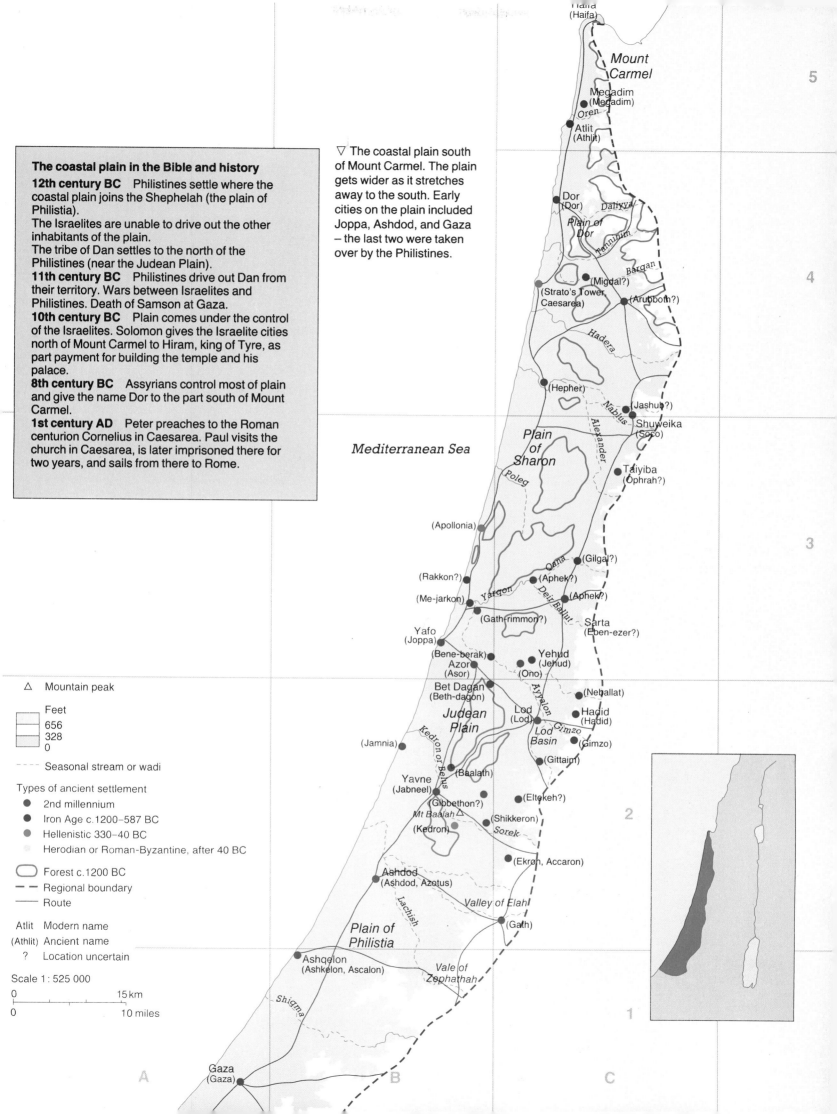

The coastal plain in the Bible and history

12th century BC Philistines settle where the coastal plain joins the Shephelah (the plain of Philistia).
The Israelites are unable to drive out the other inhabitants of the plain.
The tribe of Dan settles to the north of the Philistines (near the Judean Plain).
11th century BC Philistines drive out Dan from their territory. Wars between Israelites and Philistines. Death of Samson at Gaza.
10th century BC Plain comes under the control of the Israelites. Solomon gives the Israelite cities north of Mount Carmel to Hiram, king of Tyre, as part payment for building the temple and his palace.
8th century BC Assyrians control most of plain and give the name Dor to the part south of Mount Carmel.
1st century AD Peter preaches to the Roman centurion Cornelius in Caesarea. Paul visits the church in Caesarea, is later imprisoned there for two years, and sails from there to Rome.

▽ The coastal plain south of Mount Carmel. The plain gets wider as it stretches away to the south. Early cities on the plain included Joppa, Ashdod, and Gaza – the last two were taken over by the Philistines.

Haifa
(Haifa)

Mount Carmel

Megadim
(Megadim)

Oren

Atlit
(Athlit)

Dor
(Dor)

Daliyya

Plain of Dor

Tanninim

Bargan

Migdal?

(Strato's Tower, Caesarea)

(Arubboth?)

Hadera

(Hepher)

Nablus

Jashub?

Shuweika
(Soco)

Plain of Sharon

Alexander

Mediterranean Sea

Taiyiba
(Ophrah?)

Poleg

(Apollonia)

Qana

(Gilgal?)

(Rakkon?)

(Aphek?)

(Me-jarkon)

Yarqon

Deir Ballut

(Aphek?)

Sarta
(Eben-ezer?)

(Gath-rimmon?)

Yafo
(Joppa)

(Bene-berak)

Yehud
(Jehud)

Azor
(Asor)

(Ono)

Bet Dagan
(Beth-dagon)

Ayyalon

(Neballat)

Lod
(Lod)

Judean Plain

Gimzo

Hadid
(Hadid)

Lod Basin

(Gimzo)

(Jamnia)

Kedron or Belus

(Gittaim)

(Baalath)

Yavne
(Jabneel)

(Gibbethon?)
Mt Baalah △

(Eltekeh?)

(Shikkeron)

(Kedron)

Sorek

(Ekron, Accaron)

Ashdod
(Ashdod, Azotus)

Lachish

Valley of Elah

(Gath)

Plain of Philistia

Ashqelon
(Ashkelon, Ascalon)

Vale of Zephathah

Shiqma

Gaza
(Gaza)

△ Mountain peak

Feet
656
328
0

- - - Seasonal stream or wadi

Types of ancient settlement
● 2nd millennium
● Iron Age c.1200–587 BC
● Hellenistic 330–40 BC
 Herodian or Roman-Byzantine, after 40 BC

◯ Forest c.1200 BC
- - - Regional boundary
——— Route

Atlit Modern name
(Athlit) Ancient name
? Location uncertain

Scale 1 : 525 000

0   15 km
0   10 miles

5

4

3

2

1

A   B   C

Caesarea

The coastal plain immediately south of Mount Carmel did not have a good harbor. So Herod the Great built a new port. The work was begun in 22 BC and finished 13 years later. The new harbor town, Caesarea, became the capital of the Jewish kings and Roman governors of Judea. These included Pontius Pilate, the governor responsible for the crucifixion of Jesus.

By AD 600 Caesarea had grown very large – about 500,000 people lived there. It was damaged during the Muslim invasion of the 7th century AD, and then became a Crusader stronghold in the 12th century. The Crusaders were European Christian soldiers fighting to conquer the Holy Land.

◁ The best natural harbor on the southern coastal plain was Joppa, pictured here. Joppa was the main port of the coastal plain right up to the 20th century.

▷ This site plan of Caesarea shows the extent of Herod's capital (1st century BC), the larger Byzantine city (7th century AD), and the smaller Crusader stronghold (12th–13th centuries AD). The Crusader walls still stand.

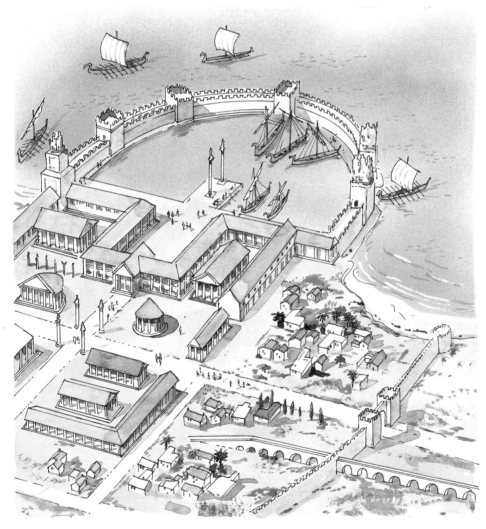

◁ An artist's view of Caesarea and its harbor as they might have looked in ancient times. The entrance to the harbor is on the right-hand side, the walls giving shelter to the boats at anchor. Two main types of boat were used for normal trade – those that kept close to shore and those that crossed the Mediterranean during favorable seasons. Close to the harbor were great storehouses. The aqueduct can be seen in the bottom right-hand corner.

▷ This massive aqueduct was built during Herod's reign to help bring water to Caesarea from the southern slopes of Mount Carmel, 5½ miles from the city. Caesarea was not near to a reliable water supply, but by this time engineering skills were able to bring water over long distances. Herod's impressive construction carried the water for the final part of its journey.

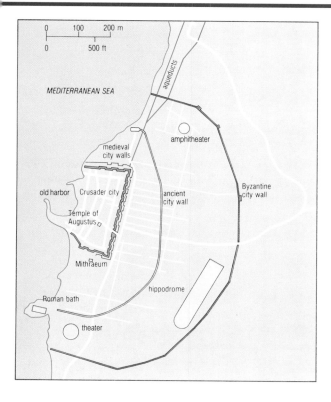

Caesarea

Christians at Caesarea

We know from Acts 21 verses 7 to 14 that there was a Christian congregation in Caesarea at the time of Paul's last visit to Jerusalem in AD 58. Paul stayed at the house of Philip the evangelist, and it was here that Paul's arrest was foretold.

In the 3rd century AD the great scholar Origen (c. 185–254) lived in Caesarea. His great work, the *Hexapla*, set out the Old Testament in Hebrew and Greek. This book was lost in the Muslim invasions; but we know of it from references by scholars. In the 4th century AD the bishop of Caesarea, Eusebius, wrote a book which tried to identify the places named in the Bible.

▽ Remains of the Crusader city. These arches date from the 13th century AD. They form a passage leading to the southeast corner of Caesarea.

THE SHEPHELAH

The Shephelah – *shephelah* is the Hebrew word for "lowlands" – is to the west of the Judean Hills. The region is about 50 mi long from north to south. It has low round hills and is crossed by several broad valleys running from west to east.

There is a big difference in rainfall between the southern end of the Shephelah (10 in of rain per year) and the northern part (20 in). So the north was more popular as a place to live in biblical times. People here grew vines and olive and fig trees.

Struggle for the land

The Shephelah belonged to the tribe of Judah. Immediately to the west were the Philistines on the coastal plain, and battles took place here between the two peoples. The most famous occasion was David's fight with the Philistine Goliath. David's skill in throwing a stone with the aid of a sling defeated the giant.

In the 8th and the 6th centuries BC the Shephelah was the scene of fighting during invasions by the Assyrians and Babylonians. The main route to Judah's second city, Lachish, passed through the region. In the reign of Hezekiah (727–698 BC) the towns along this route were turned into military fortresses – an act that a local prophet named Micah heavily criticized. However, the Israelites' precautions

▷ A typical view of the Shephelah landscape, with broad valleys and gentle hills. The land climbs upward toward the background and then joins the Judean Hills, which are about 2,000 ft higher.

▽ Lachish was the second most important city in Judah. It is shown here as it might have been in 701 BC when it was captured by the Assyrian king Sennacherib. Important towns were often defended by two rings of walls, joined together by a massive fortified gateway, as seen here. If an enemy overran the first wall, the defenders could retreat to the second line and fight again. After his victory at Lachish, Sennacherib recorded the siege on stone reliefs that are now in the British Museum.

were in vain. The Assyrians drove them out from this area when they invaded Judah in 705 BC. Lachish fell after a siege.

During excavations at Lachish in the 1930s some ancient messages written on pieces of pottery were found in the guardroom of the city gate. They had been sent from an observation post during Nebuchadnezzar's invasion of 588 BC. They tell of a time when all the Judean cities except Lachish had been captured by the Babylonians.

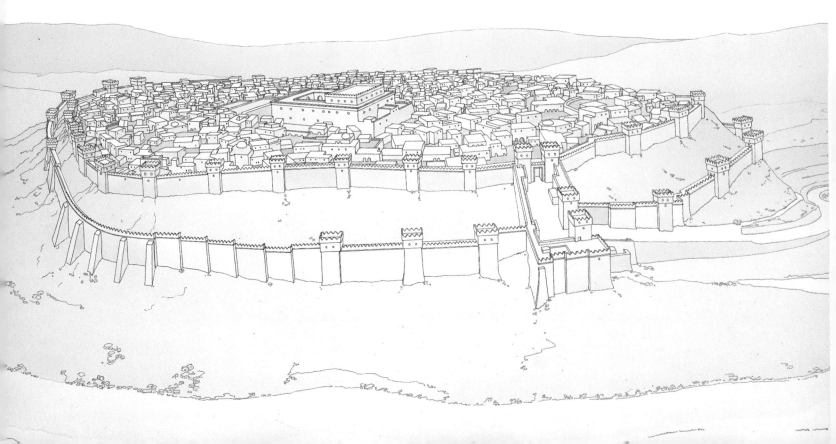

The Shephelah in the Bible and history

12th century BC Joshua captures several cities, including Lachish.

11th century BC Encounters between Samson and the Philistines in the northern Shephelah. David fights and defeats Goliath in the Valley of Elah. David sets up his base at Adullam during his flight from Saul.

10th century BC Shoshenq I, king of Egypt, invades Israel and Judah via western Shephelah.

8th century BC Amaziah, king of Judah, defeated by Joash, king of Israel, at Beth-shemesh (c.786 BC). In 705 BC Sennacherib invades Judah, drives out the people who live in the Shephelah, and captures Lachish after a siege.

6th century BC Nebuchadnezzar invades Judah in 589–588 BC. The "Lachish letters," written on pieces of pot, tell of the fall of Azekah, another fortified town.

5th century BC A Persian governor of the area has his official residence in Lachish.

▷ The Shephelah is the strip of land between the coastal plain and the Judean Hills. The main route down to Lachish divides it into a lower western and a more hilly eastern part. The valleys of the winter streams Sorek, Elah, and Lachish allow travel between east and west.

Feet
1968
656
328

- - - - Seasonal stream or wadi

Types of ancient settlement
● 2nd millennium
● Iron Age c.1200–587 BC
● Persian 587–330 BC
● Hellenistic 330–40 BC

⬭ Forest c.1200 BC

- - - Regional boundary

⸺ Route

Gezer Modern name

(azara) Ancient name

? Location uncertain

Scale 1: 250 000

0   8km

0   6 miles

Gezer
(Gezer, Gazara)
Mikerli
Nahshon
(Emmaus?, Nicopolis)
(Aijalon Elon)
(Makaz?)
(Gederah, Gederoth)
Meir
Harel
(Ashnah?)
(Timnah?)
(Zorah)
Eshtaol (Eshtaol)
Sorek
(Beer?)
Bet-Shemesh (Beth-shemesh)
(En-gannim?)
(Elon?)
Zanoah (Zanoah)
(Jarmuth)
Valley of Elah (Azekah)
(Gederothaim?)
Elah
(Soco, Socoh)
(Harim?)
(Adullam)
(Achzib, Libnah?)
(Libnah?)
(Moresheth-gath?)
(Ether)
(Nahash?)
(Keilah)
(Zenan?)
Shephelah
(Mareshah)
(Magbish?)
Guvrin
(Nezib)
(Elam?)
(Lahmam?)
(Iphtah Tricomias)
Lakhish (Lachish)
(Ashnah?)
(Cabbon?)
Lachish
(Migdal-gad?)
(Bozkath)
(Makkedah?)
(Shaphir?)
Noam
(Eglon?)
(Chitlish)
Adorayim
(Dilean)
(Eglon?)
Kelekh
(Debir?, Goshen?)
Shigma

THE JUDEAN HILLS AND DESERT

The Judean Hills, encompassing the Hebron and Bethel Hills, begin at Bethlehem in the north and extend south to the winter stream of Beer-sheba. From Bethlehem to several miles south of Hebron the hills were probably covered by evergreen oak forests with patches of pines in Old Testament times. Farther south of Hebron, with an average rainfall of 12 in per year, only shrubs and a few trees grew. As everywhere in the land of the Bible, and as is still true today, more rain fell to the north and less to the south.

The Judean Desert

The Judean Desert is not a sandy wilderness like the Sahara. It has average annual rainfall of 28 in at its northern and western point, though much less beside the Dead Sea. This is enough rain to support grasses, weeds, and flowers on which sheep and goats can feed. So during the winter, the rainy period, the desert supports sizable numbers of grazing animals.

The Judean Desert is rather like a series of large "steps" going down from the Judean Hills to the Dead Sea. Each step is a flattish piece of land a mile or two wide, and it is here that animals can graze. At the Dead Sea the desert ends in high cliffs.

Abraham and David

Both Abraham and David had close links with the Judean Hills and Desert. Abraham spent most of his time in Canaan at or near Hebron and was buried there. David came from Bethlehem. As a young shepherd, he would have grazed his sheep in the Judean Desert in the rainy winters. When he was forced to flee from Saul's court, David found safety in the desert. One of his bases was at En-gedi; and he must have known the rocky plateau of Masada.

John, Jesus, and the Dead Sea scrolls

John the Baptist and Jesus spent time in the Judean Desert. They probably stayed in the north, close to where the river Jordan enters the Dead Sea. There was a religious community near here at Qumran. Some of these people's writings, the Dead Sea scrolls, were first found in 1947. John and Jesus must have been aware of the community at Qumran, but they were not members of it.

△ The Judean Hills and their narrow valleys. This modern view gives a poor impression of what the area looked like in Old Testament times. Then the hills were thickly forested; today there are only small shrubs. On the left especially, traces are visible of the farming terraces made after the trees had been cleared.

▽ This strange landscape in the Judean Desert is the result of rain and wind erosion over thousands of years. Bare in summer, in the rainy winter these hills can be covered by flowers and grasses and provide food for animals. Some plants can be seen growing at the bottom left of the photograph. A path leads in from the left.

▷ The Judean Hills and Desert. Cities such as Bethlehem and Hebron were not far from the desert. Other towns, such as Carmel and Maon to the southeast of the Judean Hills, were centers for the large flocks of sheep and goats that grazed in the desert in winter. Towns grew up around springs on the Dead Sea shore.

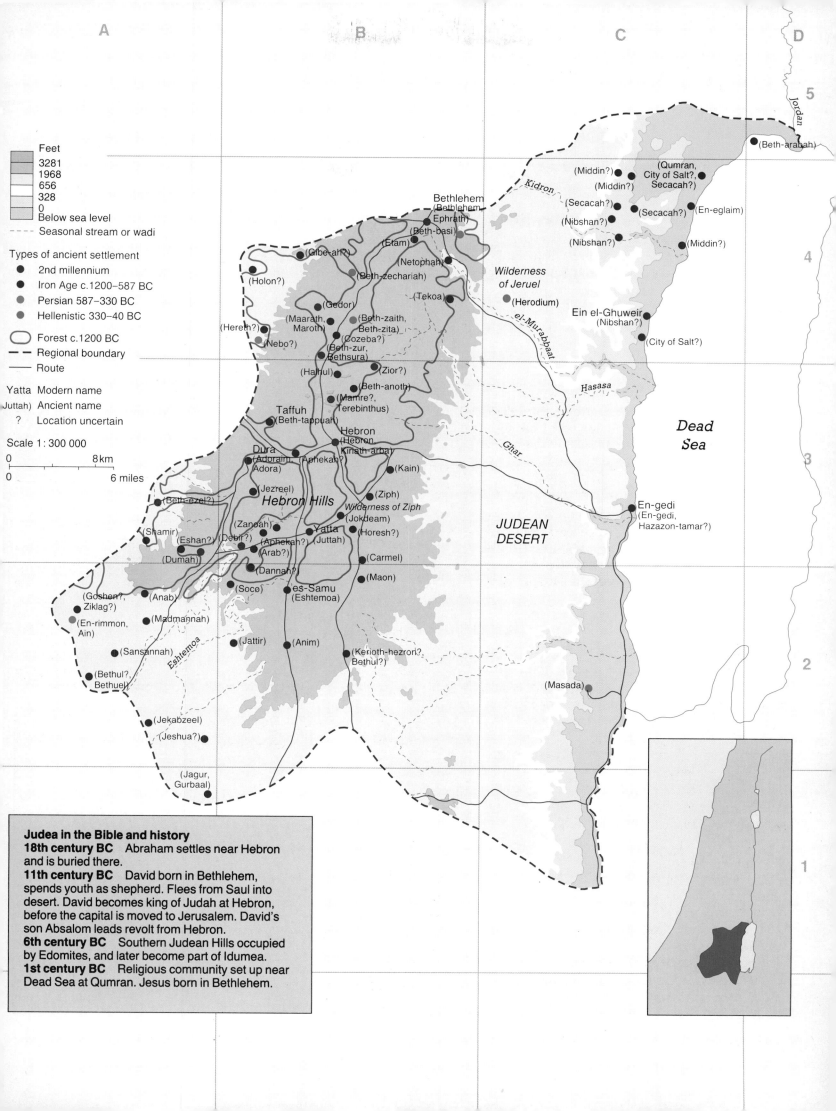

A
B
C
D

5

4

3

2

1

Feet
3281
1968
656
328
0
Below sea level
--- Seasonal stream or wadi

Types of ancient settlement
● 2nd millennium
● Iron Age c.1200–587 BC
● Persian 587–330 BC
● Hellenistic 330–40 BC

◯ Forest c.1200 BC
--- Regional boundary
— Route

Yatta Modern name
(Juttah) Ancient name
? Location uncertain

Scale 1 : 300 000

0   8km
0   6 miles

Bethlehem
(Bethlehem,
Ephrath)
(Beth-basi)
(Etam)
(Gibe-ah?)
(Netophah)
(Holon?)
(Beth-zechariah)
(Gedor)
(Maarath,
Maroth)
(Herath?)
(Beth-zaith,
Beth-zita)
(Cozeba?)
(Nebo?)
(Beth-zur,
Bethsura)
(Halhul)
(Zior?)
(Beth-anoth)
(Mamre?,
Terebinthus)
Taffuh
(Beth-tappuah)
Hebron
(Hebron,
Kiriath-arba)
Dura
(Adoraim,
Adora)
(Aphekah?)
(Kain)
(Jezreel)
(Beth-ezel?)
(Ziph)
Hebron Hills
Wilderness of Ziph
(Jokdeam)
(Zanoah)
Yatta
(Juttah)
(Horesh?)
(Shamir)
(Eshan?)
(Debir?)
(Aphekah?)
(Arab?)
(Dumah)
(Dannah?)
(Carmel)
(Soco)
(Maon)
es-Samu
(Eshtemoa)
(Goshen?,
Ziklag?)
(Anab)
(En-rimmon,
Ain)
(Madmannah)
(Jattir)
(Anim)
(Sansannah)
(Kerioth-hezron?,
Bethul?)
Eshtemoa
(Bethul?,
Bethuel)
(Masada)
(Jekabzeel)
(Jeshua?)
(Jagur,
Gurbaal)

Kidron
(Middin?)
(Middin?)
(Qumran,
City of Salt?,
Secacah?)
(Secacah?)
(Secacah?)
(En-eglaim)
(Nibshan?)
(Nibshan?)
(Middin?)
Wilderness
of Jeruel
(Herodium)
el-Murabbaat
Ein el-Ghuweir
(Nibshan?)
(City of Salt?)
Hasasa
Ghar
**Dead
Sea**
En-gedi
(En-gedi,
Hazazon-tamar?)
JUDEAN
DESERT

Jordan
(Beth-arabah)

Judea in the Bible and history
18th century BC Abraham settles near Hebron
and is buried there.
11th century BC David born in Bethlehem,
spends youth as shepherd. Flees from Saul into
desert. David becomes king of Judah at Hebron,
before the capital is moved to Jerusalem. David's
son Absalom leads revolt from Hebron.
6th century BC Southern Judean Hills occupied
by Edomites, and later become part of Idumea.
1st century BC Religious community set up near
Dead Sea at Qumran. Jesus born in Bethlehem.

Masada

Masada lies on a steep-sided flat-topped hill, 1,345 ft above the shore of the Dead Sea. Its name means "fortress" in Hebrew. The plateau (level ground) at the top is 656 yd long and 350 yd wide. The steep cliffs on all sides make it very difficult to attack.

Although Masada is not mentioned in the Bible, it is almost certain that David knew it. During his flight from the court of Saul, David was almost captured by Saul near "the rock . . . in the wilderness of Maon" (1 Samuel chapter 23 verses 25 to 27). David escaped because Saul received news of a Philistine attack that he had to deal with. This rock may well have been Masada.

Remains found at Masada show that people lived on the rock from the 10th to the 7th centuries BC. It was not until 100 BC, however, that it was made into a fortress. Masada did not have a water supply, and the region had very low rainfall. Only when engineers could build huge caverns to trap

▽ This is thought to be the site of the synagogue (place of Jewish worship) at Masada – the oldest such site known to archaeologists and historians. Traces of a Roman siege camp are in the distant valley on the right.

▷ This view from the air shows how Masada has steep slopes on all sides. The Roman camps and siege ramp are on the left. On the right a path winds its way to the top. The Judean Desert stretches out in the background.

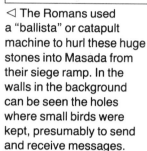

and keep the rainwater could Masada become a permanent fortress.

Masada, as we can see it today, was built by Herod the Great to be one of his winter palaces. At the northern end, where the rock went down in three steps, Herod had his royal palace and a private villa, complete with a bath house.

During the revolt of the Jews against Rome in AD 67–73, Masada became a fortress once again. Here the rebels made their last stand before the Romans broke into their stronghold by building a huge ramp to make their attack on the western side.

◁ The Romans used a "ballista" or catapult machine to hurl these huge stones into Masada from their siege ramp. In the walls in the background can be seen the holes where small birds were kept, presumably to send and receive messages.

◁ Masada as it might have looked during the Roman siege. The Romans made their attack from the west (right of picture), where Herod had built a defensive gate and tower. First they built a sloping ramp then they moved their siege machines up the ramp to within firing range of the fortress. Most of the buildings at Masada were at the northern end of the plateau (center of picture). The siege ended when all the defenders – men, women, and children – committed suicide. In all it took almost two years for 15,000 Roman soldiers to subdue the fortress, fighting against less than 1,000 men, women and children.

Qumran

Like Masada, Qumran is not mentioned in the Bible, unless it was the site of Secacah or the City of Salt (Joshua 15 verses 61 to 62). It has become famous since 1947 by being associated with the Dead Sea scrolls. (A scroll is a roll of paper, parchment, or other writing material.)

Discovery of the Dead Sea scrolls

The first of the scrolls was discovered by an Arab boy in a cave about a mile north of Qumran in 1947. Qumran was not at first thought to be an important site; but as more scrolls were found, people decided to excavate the area. As a result, we now know that a religious group – possibly the group called the Essenes – lived at Qumran in the 1st centuries BC and AD. Some pieces of scrolls were found very close to Qumran, and it is possible that the scrolls were written in one of the rooms there.

Scrolls were found in 13 caves at the northern end of the Dead Sea. Some had been wrapped in leather and placed in jars. One was inscribed on copper that had then been beaten into a scroll. It was a list of buried treasure, and it was cut open strip by strip at the University of Manchester.

The writings on the scrolls and the pieces of scroll are of two kinds. Some contain parts of the Bible. The others tell us about the organization, beliefs, and worship of the Qumran community. The Qumran manuscripts of the Old Testament are the oldest that we now have.

The community at Qumran

Did the Qumran community own and hide all the scrolls that have been found? If so, why did they hide some of them a mile away? These people are thought to have lived a life of Bible study, prayer, and worship. Their Hebrew name meant "the sons of light." They believed that most Jews did not obey God's laws correctly. But they were closer to God's will and had a key part to play in defeating the evil "sons of darkness."

◁ Some of the Dead Sea scrolls were placed in jars such as these. This suggests that these scrolls were worn out with use and then carefully stored away. In the Jewish religion, scrolls containing the Bible must not be destroyed.

▽ A view from one of the caves where scrolls or pieces of scroll were found. While some scrolls were reasonably well preserved, in many cases only hundreds of small pieces were found.

Herodium

Herodium is a huge man-made mound in the Judean Hills close to the Judean Desert. From the top of it there are magnificent views of the desert. Its distinctive shape was the result of earth being heaped up around a very large circular tower – under the orders of Herod the Great.

Herod's monument

In about 40 BC King Herod was forced to flee from Jerusalem when the land was invaded by the Parthians. Herod's enemies in Judea took the opportunity to try to overthrow him. When the two sides met in battle at a site about 7½ mi from Jerusalem, Herod was victorious. Some years later the king marked the place of his victory by building a summer palace there named after himself.

At the top of the artificial mound Herod surrounded his palace with a double wall with four towers at the four points of the compass. Next to the eastern tower was a large garden. On the western side were the palace buildings, several stories high. Water was stored in large cisterns beneath the buildings. People entered the fortified palace by a staircase between the northern and eastern towers. There were many tunnels.

Herodium in history

Herodium is not mentioned in the Bible, though it was completed before the birth of Jesus. In 15 BC Herod entertained Marcus Agrippa, a close friend of the Roman emperor, at a number of places including Herodium. He also left instructions that he should be buried there, though his tomb has not been found. In the Jewish revolts against Rome of AD 67–73 and 132–5 Jewish fighters occupied Herodium but then lost it to the Romans. On the second occasion the buildings were badly damaged.

Qumran •
Herodium •

▽ View of Herodium from the air, with the Judean Desert in the background. Within the mound it is possible to see the pillars that surrounded the garden. The remains of the large eastern tower are slightly above the left-hand side, and the sites of the other towers can just be made out. At the foot of the mound are the results of excavations of other buildings.

THE NEGEV AND SINAI

The Negev is the dry region in the south of Israel, beyond the Hebron Hills. The part southwest of the city of Beer-sheba is very sandy. But to the southeast there are mountains over 3,000 ft high and some spectacular craters of which the largest is 25 mi by 5 mi.

The Sinai Desert is three times as big as the Negev, covering about 11,000 square mi. It reaches from the Mediterranean Sea in the north to the Red Sea in the south.

Beer-sheba

The main town in the Negev was Beer-sheba. This stood on the main routes from the Negev to the coastal plain, the Shephelah, the Hebron Hills, and the valley below the Dead Sea. It had wells (the name Beer-sheba may mean "plentiful well" or perhaps "seven wells"), and the townspeople channeled the winter rains into storage caves. Beer-sheba is an important place in the stories of Abraham, Isaac, and Jacob.

Kadesh-barnea

In the western Negev, close to where Sinai commences, is Kadesh-barnea. The Israelites stayed here while journeying from Egypt to the Promised Land of Israel. From Kadesh 12 spies were sent out to see what the Promised Land was like. Ten of the spies said that they did not like it, and God decided that the Israelites would have to wait longer to enter it.

It was also at Kadesh that the people complained that they did not have enough water. Moses had to produce water by striking a rock with his stick. Kadesh is mentioned in the Old Testament as a place where the Israelites doubted if God would bring them safely to a land of their own.

Mount Sinai

The Old Testament says that the Israelites spent 40 years wandering in the Sinai Desert and the Negev. The place of greatest importance in the desert was Mount Sinai. On this, Moses received the Ten Commandments from God, and God and the people entered into a covenant (a special agreement). The Israelites were to be a special people in God's eyes because he had rescued them from slavery in Egypt. In return, they had to live in obedience to the laws God gave them.

◁ A view of the Sinai desert. Here a sandy landscape with small shrubs is bordered by rugged mountains. Camels can travel for long distances over this area without water – but the Israelites did not have camels.

▽ One of the spectacular craters in the Negev, at a place near Mount Zin. The rocks have been worn away by wind and rain after originally being forced up to the earth's surface by pressure from beneath.

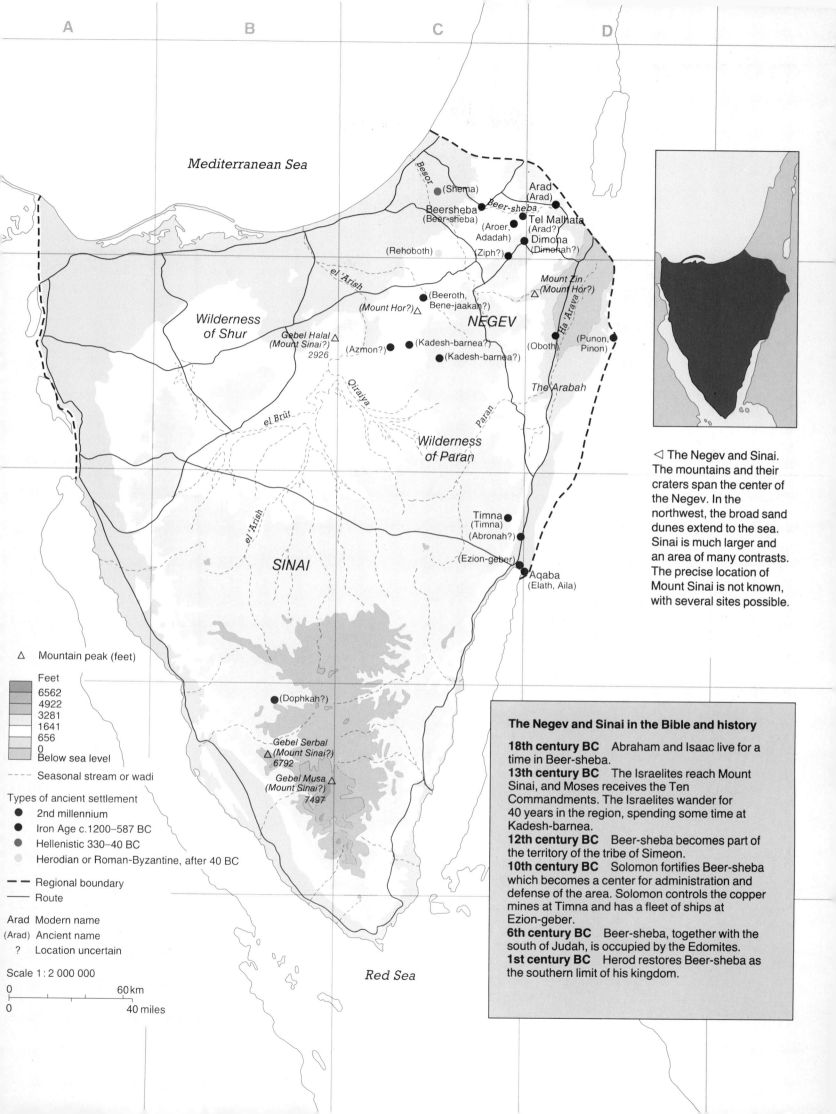

Mediterranean Sea

Besor

● (Shema)

Arad
(Arad)

Beersheba
(Beer-sheba)

Beer-sheba

Tel Malhata
(Arad?)

(Aroer,
Adadah)

Dimona
(Dimonah?)

(Rehoboth)

(Ziph?)

el 'Arish

*Mount Zin
(Mount Hor?)*
△

(Beeroth,
Bene-jaakan?)

(Mount Hor?) △

NEGEV

Ha 'Arava

Gebel Halal △
(Mount Sinai?)
2926

(Azmon?) ● ● (Kadesh-barnea?)

(Kadesh-barnea?) ●

(Oboth) ●

(Punon,
Pinon)

Wilderness
of Shur

The Arabah

Qiraiya

el Brût

Wilderness
of Paran

Paran

el 'Arish

Timna
(Timna)

(Abronah?)

(Ezion-geber)

Aqaba
(Elath, Aila)

SINAI

● (Dophkah?)

Gebel Serbal
△ (Mount Sinai?)
6792

Gebel Musa
(Mount Sinai?) △
7497

Red Sea

◁ The Negev and Sinai.
The mountains and their
craters span the center of
the Negev. In the
northwest, the broad sand
dunes extend to the sea.
Sinai is much larger and
an area of many contrasts.
The precise location of
Mount Sinai is not known,
with several sites possible.

△   Mountain peak (feet)

Feet
6562
4922
3281
1641
656
0
Below sea level

– – –   Seasonal stream or wadi

Types of ancient settlement
●   2nd millennium
●   Iron Age c.1200–587 BC
●   Hellenistic 330–40 BC
○   Herodian or Roman-Byzantine, after 40 BC

━ ━ ━   Regional boundary
———   Route

Arad   Modern name
(Arad)   Ancient name
?   Location uncertain

Scale 1 : 2 000 000

0   60 km

0   40 miles

The Negev and Sinai in the Bible and history

18th century BC   Abraham and Isaac live for a
time in Beer-sheba.
13th century BC   The Israelites reach Mount
Sinai, and Moses receives the Ten
Commandments. The Israelites wander for
40 years in the region, spending some time at
Kadesh-barnea.
12th century BC   Beer-sheba becomes part of
the territory of the tribe of Simeon.
10th century BC   Solomon fortifies Beer-sheba
which becomes a center for administration and
defense of the area. Solomon controls the copper
mines at Timna and has a fleet of ships at
Ezion-geber.
6th century BC   Beer-sheba, together with the
south of Judah, is occupied by the Edomites.
1st century BC   Herod restores Beer-sheba as
the southern limit of his kingdom.

Arad

Arad was two towns in ancient times. There was an older, lower town, where people lived before the biblical period. There was also a later, upper town, dating from the 12th or 11th century BC. According to Numbers chapter 21 verses 1 to 3, the Israelites conquered Arad in the 13th century BC. We cannot be sure whether the Bible is referring to the site we know as Arad or to another town in the area known as Tel Malhata.

During the reign of Solomon, Arad became a fortified city. But it was destroyed soon afterward when the Egyptian Pharaoh Shoshenq I invaded the land in 924 BC. In the following centuries Arad was wrecked and rebuilt many times. This was because of its important position on the route along the foot of the Hebron Hills to the Jordan valley.

Among the interesting finds at Arad were the site of a temple and letters written on pieces of broken pot.

△ A seal of Eliashib, a commander of Arad in the 7th or 6th century BC. The seal was pressed on clay when the officer sent instructions.

▽ Plan of Arad. The temple, in the top left corner, seems to have had the same layout as Solomon's temple in Jerusalem. But it may have been built later.

Beer-sheba

The name Beer-sheba is closely connected in the Bible with stories about Abraham and Isaac. These founders of the Israelite people, however, were not city dwellers; they lived in tents and traveled with their sheep and goats. The ancient site that can be seen at Beer-sheba today dates from a later period.

The remains at Beer-sheba are from the city built at the end of the 11th century BC and then fortified by Solomon. As in the case of Arad, the town was probably destroyed by Shoshenq I in 924 BC. After being rebuilt, it was the most important town on Judah's southern border. A road ran all the way round it, inside the city walls. When the Bible speaks about the whole of the land of Israel, it often refers to the land from Dan (in the far north) to Beer-sheba. The Assyrian king Sennacherib is thought to have attacked the town in 701 BC; after this it never regained its former glory.

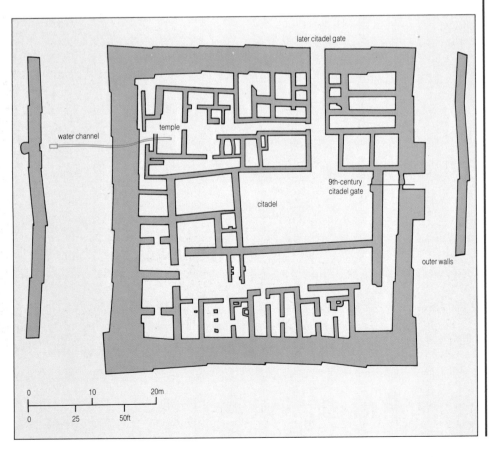

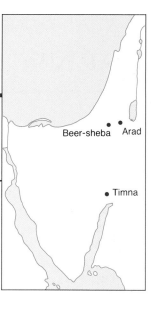

Timna

Copper was mined at Timna as long ago as 4000 BC. Mining was begun again in the 13th century BC. Soon afterward the Egyptians used the site, building a temple there to their goddess Hathor. Then Timna was taken over by people from the land of Midian, to the east of Sinai.

In the Bible, Moses marries a Midianite woman and spends time in the wilderness of Midian after killing an Egyptian and fleeing from the Egyptian court. (The Egyptian had been beating a Hebrew slave.) At Timna a Midianite place of worship has been found that was covered by a tent – similar to the tent-shrine that Moses commanded the Israelites to make.

Another biblical connection is the story in Numbers chapter 21 verses 6 to 9 about the Israelites setting up a snake made of copper on a pole: a copper snake was found in the Midianite temple at Timna.

△ Beer-sheba's famous camel market. For centuries the town has been a center for the Bedouin, the Arabs who live with their camels in the Negev and Sinai. Now it is also a thriving modern university city.

▽ A view from the air of the remains of the first city of Beer-sheba, built in the 11th century BC. In the foreground is the bed of the winter stream, the Nahal Beer-sheba. The town in the distance to the left is not the modern Beer-sheba, which is out of sight of the picture, but the small settlement of Omer.

▽ Some of the rocks where copper was found at Timna. The miners made shafts into the rock to get at the metal ore. During the reigns of David and Solomon, the Israelites took control of Timna and its copper mines.

GALILEE

The name "Galilee" comes from the Hebrew word *galil* which means a district. In Old Testament Hebrew it is always known as "the Galilee." Possibly the name was short for "the district (Galilee) of the other nations (non-Israelites)", because for long periods many non-Israelites lived here.

From the 8th century BC Galilee belonged to the Israelites' enemies. The area came under Israelite control again 100 years before Jesus' birth and is important in the New Testament as the place where Jesus lived and worked.

Upper and lower Galilee

Galilee is divided into two parts, of which the northern part, upper Galilee, is the higher. It is dominated by the Meron Mountains; these run for 6.2 mi from north to south and reach heights of over 3,000 ft. There are also other mountain ranges here.

This part of Israel was thickly forested in the time of the Bible, and it still has a few remains of the ancient forests. It was difficult to travel or to live in the region. Despite its beauty, upper Galilee is rarely mentioned in the Bible.

Lower Galilee is less mountainous and has many large valleys which were cleared of trees and used for growing crops. At its southern end it joins the Valley of Jezreel, while to the east it slopes down to meet the Sea of Galilee.

There is at least one extinct volcano in lower Galilee, near to the Sea of Galilee. The lava that it once threw out remains widespread in the landscape in the form of hard black stone known as basalt. People used this basalt for building and to make grinding wheels and olive presses.

The Sea of Galilee

The Sea of Galilee is an inland lake 12½ mi long and up to 8¼ mi wide. The river Jordan enters it at the northern end and leaves it from the south. The lake surface is 689 ft below sea level. Surrounded by mountains, it can be stormy. In New Testament times many towns stood around the lake shores. Among the industries that flourished were fishing, dyeing cloth, and making olive and wine presses.

To the north of the Sea of Galilee the upper Jordan valley runs for 10½ mi before broadening into the Huleh valley with its lake.

▽ Mount Tabor is an isolated hill in lower Galilee whose peak is 1,929 ft above sea level. In the Old Testament it was a place where the tribes met when they had to face an enemy. It is also believed to be the site of Jesus' transfiguration – when his face and clothes shone with light while he prayed.

Galilee in the Bible and history

?18th century BC   Abraham pursues a group of kings who have captured his nephew, Lot, as far as the town of Dan.

13th century BC   Joshua defeats the Canaanites by the Waters of Merom and destroys the town of Hazor.

11th century BC   Israelite tribes in the north meet at Mount Tabor and defeat the Canaanites, who are led by Sisera.

9th century BC   Israel loses large areas of Galilee to the Syrians.

8th century BC   The Assyrians make Galilee part of their empire.

2nd century BC   The Judean prince Aristobulus reconquers Galilee for the Jews.

1st century AD   Jesus lives in Nazareth for 30 years before beginning his public ministry, most of which is in Galilee.

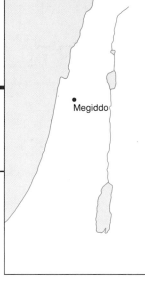

possibly killed the king during fighting outside Megiddo but could not seize the city itself. It was probably the Philistines who captured Megiddo from the Canaanites and made it a wealthy city in the 12th and 11th centuries BC. This Philistine city was violently destroyed, probably by David.

City of Solomon and Ahab

Megiddo was strongly fortified by Solomon, and remains of his work can be seen today. Solomon made Megiddo the center of one of the 12 districts into which he divided his kingdom. The Egyptian Pharaoh Shoshenq attacked and probably destroyed Megiddo in 924 BC. In the 9th century BC Omri and his son Ahab rebuilt the city. The remains of Ahab's building work at Megiddo are the so-called stables – which may have been food stores – and the water system. The water tunnel allowed people to get to the water supply at the foot of the mound without going outside the city.

Death of two kings

Two kings of Judah died at or near Megiddo. In the 8th century BC Ahaziah was wounded by King Jehu of Israel in battle and fled to Megiddo, where he died. In the 7th century BC Josiah was killed near the city by the Egyptian Neco II when he tried to stop Neco going to help Assyria against Babylon.

▽ This artist's impression of Solomon's gate at Megiddo shows the main gate at right angles to the city walls. If an enemy broke through the first gate they could still be attacked from the walls with arrows and stones. The steps at the bottom of the picture lead to a water channel.

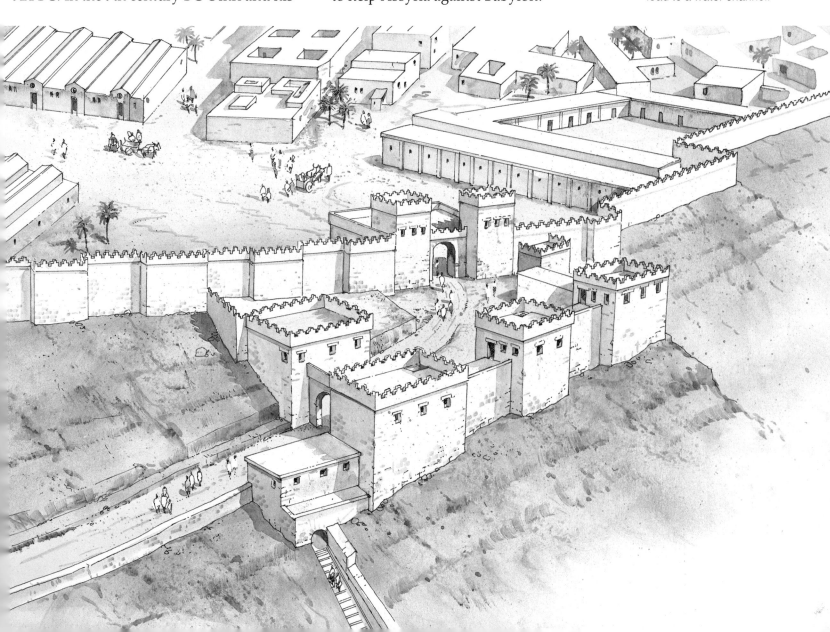

THE JERUSALEM HILLS

The Jerusalem Hills form a "saddle" (a lower piece of land) within the Judean Hills. They lie between the Bethel Hills to the north and the Hebron Hills to the south. They cover an area about 12½ mi long from north to south, and the hills are about 650 ft lower than the highest of the Bethel and Hebron hills. In the north is a plain on which a small airport has been built.

The eastern side of the Jerusalem Hills borders the Judean Desert. Valleys on the western side lead toward the coastal plain.

Links with the Old Testament
Gibeon was one of the major cities in the Jerusalem Hills. Its inhabitants saved their city from destruction by Joshua by playing a trick on him. They met him not far from the city pretending to have traveled a long distance; then they made an agreement with him. Later, Solomon worshipped God at Gibeon before he built the temple in Jerusalem.

The territory of the tribe of Benjamin was in the Jerusalem Hills; and Israel's first king, Saul, had his capital at Gibeah. He and his son Jonathan fought battles with the Philistines near Michmash.

Another important town was Mizpah, where Saul's appointment as king was confirmed. Mizpah became the main city of Judah for a while after the Babylonians destroyed Jerusalem in 587–586 BC. The prophet Jeremiah belonged to the tribe of Benjamin and came from the village of Anathoth, 3 mi north of Jerusalem.

Importance in the New Testament
Two places apart from Jerusalem are important in the New Testament. The first is Bethany, to the east of Jerusalem. Lazarus and his sisters Martha and Mary lived here, and one of Jesus' miracles took place in Bethany when he restored Lazarus to life. During the last week of his life Jesus stayed in Bethany each night.

The second important place is Emmaus, to which the risen Jesus walked with two disciples, who did not recognize him. However, we do not know where Emmaus was; there are four possible sites.

▷ The Jerusalem Hills. Jerusalem is in the southeast and stands where many important routes meet. Routes from the coastal plain and the Shephelah can be clearly seen. The forest areas show how the land probably was in about 1200 BC. By Jesus' time many of the forests had gone.

◁ The modern village of Anata is thought to be the site of Anathoth, the village where Jeremiah lived. The landscape here has lost all its trees. The terraces were built for farming – especially perhaps for largescale grape growing – after the trees had been removed. The earliest terraces date from the 10th century BC and were used for over 1,500 years.

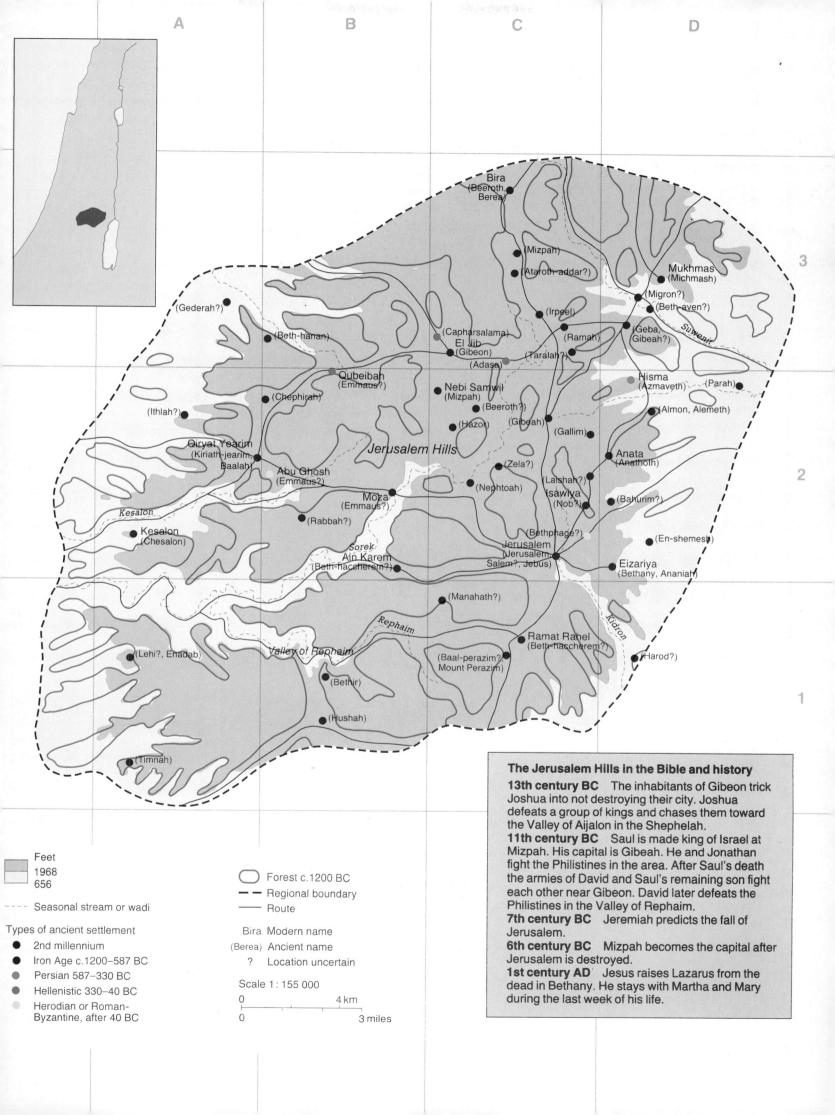

A   B   C   D

Bira
(Beeroth,
Berea)

(Mizpah)

(Ataroth-addar?)

Mukhmas
(Michmash)

(Migron?)

(Beth-aven?)

(Irpeel)

(Gederah?)

Geba,
Gibeah?)

Suweni

(Ramah)

(Beth-hanan)

(Capharsalama)

El Jib
(Gibeon)

(Taralah?)

(Adasa)

Qubeibah
(Emmaus?)

Nebi Samwil
(Mizpah)

Hisma
(Azmaveth)

(Parah)

(Chephirah)

(Beeroth?)

(Almon, Alemeth)

(Ithlah?)

(Hazor)

(Gibeah)

(Gallim)

Jerusalem Hills

Qiryat Yearim
(Kiriath-jearim,
Baalah)

Anata
(Anathoth)

(Zela)

Abu Ghosh
(Emmaus?)

(Laishah?)

Isawiya
(Nob?)

(Bahurim?)

(Nephtoah)

Moza
(Emmaus?)

Kesalon

(Rabbah?)

Kesalon
(Chesalon)

Sorek

(En-shemesh)

(Bethphage?)

Ain Karem
(Beth-haccherem?)

Jerusalem
(Jerusalem,
Salem?, Jebus)

Eizariya
(Bethany, Ananiah)

(Manahath?)

Rephaim

Kidron

Valley of Rephaim

Ramat Rahel
(Beth-haccherem?)

(Lehi?, Enadab)

(Baal-perazim?,
Mount Perazim)

(Harod?)

(Bethir)

(Hushah)

(Timnah)

Legend

Feet
1968
656

- - - Seasonal stream or wadi

Types of ancient settlement
- 2nd millennium
- Iron Age c.1200–587 BC
- Persian 587–330 BC
- Hellenistic 330–40 BC
- Herodian or Roman-
Byzantine, after 40 BC

◯ Forest c.1200 BC
- - - Regional boundary
—— Route

Bira   Modern name
(Berea)   Ancient name
?   Location uncertain

Scale 1 : 155 000

0   4 km

0   3 miles

The Jerusalem Hills in the Bible and history

13th century BC   The inhabitants of Gibeon trick Joshua into not destroying their city. Joshua defeats a group of kings and chases them toward the Valley of Aijalon in the Shephelah.

11th century BC   Saul is made king of Israel at Mizpah. His capital is Gibeah. He and Jonathan fight the Philistines in the area. After Saul's death the armies of David and Saul's remaining son fight each other near Gibeon. David later defeats the Philistines in the Valley of Rephaim.

7th century BC   Jeremiah predicts the fall of Jerusalem.

6th century BC   Mizpah becomes the capital after Jerusalem is destroyed.

1st century AD   Jesus raises Lazarus from the dead in Bethany. He stays with Martha and Mary during the last week of his life.

OLD TESTAMENT JERUSALEM

Ancient Jerusalem was surprisingly small. The city stood on a thumb-shaped spur or ridge with valleys on three sides, connected to hills only at the northern end. It was lower than the hills around it. But it had one vital thing that they lacked: a spring of water that flowed throughout the year.

The city of David

Jerusalem was at least 1,500 years old before David captured it and made it his capital. The first mention of the place in the Bible is in the story of Abraham, when he met the king of Salem (probably Jerusalem) after he had rescued his nephew Lot from kings from the north (see Genesis chapter 14).

The Israelites did not conquer the city before the time of David. Jerusalem was said to be so well fortified that it could be defended by blind and lame people. How David took it is not known – possibly he sent his army up the water shaft. Solomon extended the city to the north and built the temple and his palace.

Growth in the 8th century BC

The defeat of the northern kingdom of Israel by the Assyrians in 722 BC caused many people to flee south. We know that Jerusalem grew considerably at this time. People began to build on the western hill. In 705 BC King Hezekiah rebelled against the Assyrians and fortified the city in readiness for battle. He built an underground water tunnel so that, while the Assyrians would find no water outside Jerusalem, people in the city would be well supplied. You can walk through much of this tunnel today.

Destruction and rebuilding

Despite its strong defenses, Jerusalem fell to the Babylonians in 597 and 587–586 BC. On the second occasion the temple was destroyed and the walls were pulled down. In 539 BC the Persians allowed the Jews to rebuild their city and temple; but the work was slow, and the new temple was only a poor shadow of the one Solomon had built.

When Nehemiah, a favorite servant of the Persian king Artaxerxes I, visited Jerusalem in 445 BC he found the city in a sorry state. Nehemiah went on to help organize further rebuilding.

◁ The modern entrance to Hezekiah's water tunnel. From the steps a series of channels that were built before the time of David lead into the tunnel proper. Two gangs of miners built the tunnel working from opposite directions.

▽ Jars excavated from the city of King David.

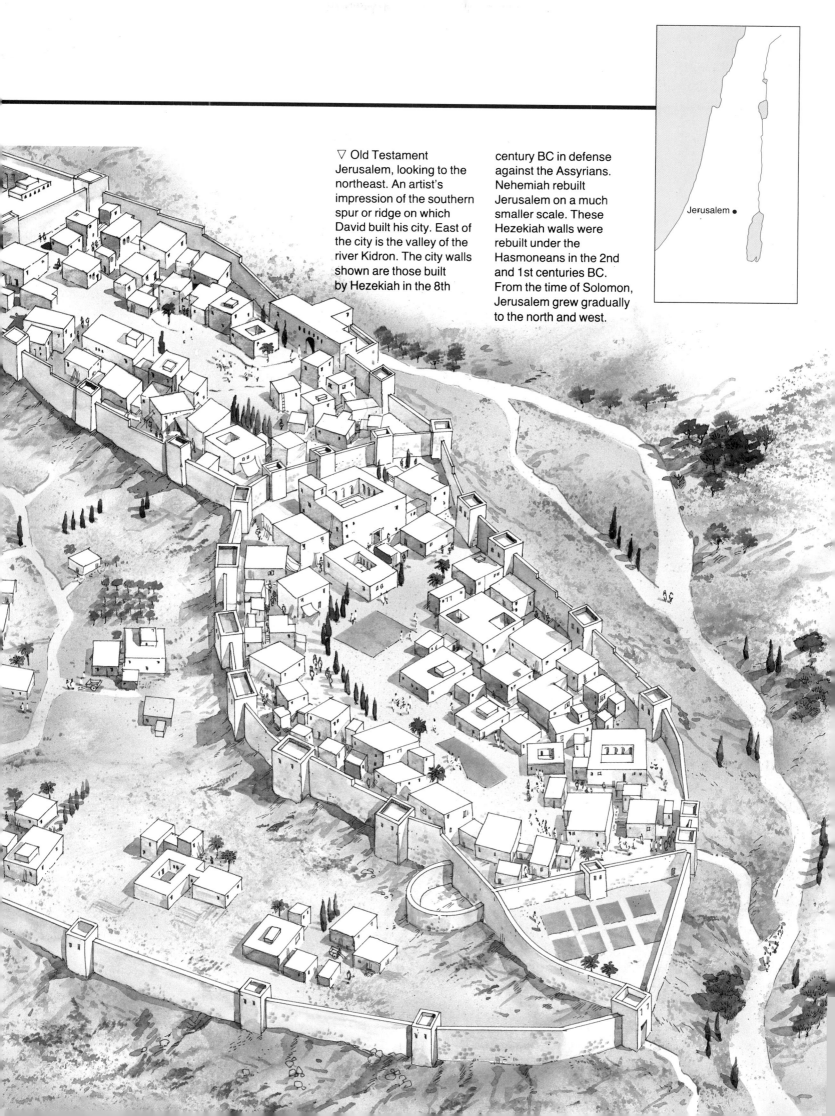

▽ Old Testament Jerusalem, looking to the northeast. An artist's impression of the southern spur or ridge on which David built his city. East of the city is the valley of the river Kidron. The city walls shown are those built by Hezekiah in the 8th century BC in defense against the Assyrians. Nehemiah rebuilt Jerusalem on a much smaller scale. These Hezekiah walls were rebuilt under the Hasmoneans in the 2nd and 1st centuries BC. From the time of Solomon, Jerusalem grew gradually to the north and west.

Jerusalem ●

NEW TESTAMENT JERUSALEM

New Testament Jerusalem was very different from the struggling city that Nehemiah did his best to strengthen in 445 BC. Since that time it had been rebuilt and had grown. The Jerusalem that Jesus knew was mainly the work of Herod the Great.

Herod's Jerusalem

At the top of the western hill stood Herod's upper palace. It had three towers and was laid out with gardens and pools. After AD 6 Judea was ruled directly by the Romans, and the Roman governor used this palace whenever he was in Jerusalem. Down the slope from the palace, Jerusalem's richer inhabitants had their big fine houses. Flights of steps enabled people to get up and down the western hills, and a bridge crossed directly from the hill to the temple.

To the north of Herod's temple was the great Antonia fortress. Here, in Jesus' time, lived the Roman soldiers who were responsible for maintaining the peace and Roman rule.

Ancient Jerusalem – the city of David on the spur – had become less important than before. It still had its defensive walls, but its houses were probably poor compared with those on the western hill.

We do not know exactly where all the city walls were, especially those to the north of Herod's upper palace. Jerusalem's defenses were rebuilt farther to the north as time went on. This is why people visiting Jerusalem today find the city of David *outside* the (later) city walls and the place where Jesus was nailed to the cross *inside* the walls.

Jerusalem after the time of Jesus

Jerusalem was captured and destroyed by the Romans in AD 70 during the Jewish rebellion of AD 67–73. Herod's temple was left in ruins and has never been rebuilt. Where it stood there is now a Muslim holy place, the beautiful Dome of the Rock; this was completed 1,300 years ago, in AD 692.

Another Jewish revolt broke out against the Romans in AD 132–5. The emperor Hadrian (who also erected the Roman wall in northern Britain) afterward rebuilt Jerusalem as a Roman city. The Old City of Jerusalem has retained the basic Roman plan to this day.

▽ A street scene from Jerusalem, during the New Testament period. For most of the 1st century AD Judea was ruled directly by a high official of the Roman empire, such as Pontius Pilate during Jesus' later life. Here, a Roman centurion and two accompanying soldiers confront two Jewish citizens. Many Jews hated the Romans.

◁ The remains of the pools of Bethesda, near St Stephen's gate. At the bottom of the excavations is the level of Jerusalem as it was in Jesus' time. Several churches were built over the pools, supported by the stone columns shown in the picture.

△ The pool of Siloam is at one end of Hezekiah's tunnel. In Jesus' day there were two pools – one at the bottom of the spur of the city of David and the other, shown here, higher up on the west side of the spur.

◁ The so-called pillar of Absalom in the valley to the east of Jerusalem is one of the few sights remaining that Jesus would have seen. Absalom was the son of David who rebelled against his father and in whose memory a pillar was set up; but this monument is in fact unconnected with him. It marks the tomb of a rich family buried in the 2nd century BC.

THE JORDAN VALLEY AND THE DEAD SEA

From the southern end of the Sea of Galilee the river Jordan continues its journey south. The direct distance from the Sea of Galilee to the Dead Sea is about 65 mi. But the Jordan twists and turns so much that its length between these points is much greater – about 200 mi. The Jordan is never more than 102 ft wide or 10 ft deep. So it is *not*, in the words of the popular hymn, "deep and wide."

From Galilee to Jericho
Just south of the Sea of Galilee the river Yarmuk joins the Jordan from the northeast. South of this are two important valleys on the western side. The first is the Harod valley, which leads into the Valley of Jezreel and was guarded by the great city of Beth-shean in Old Testament times. Here the bodies of Saul and his sons were displayed by the Philistines after the battle on nearby Mount Gilboa. The second valley is the Faria valley, which has a good route to Shechem in the Samaria Hills.

At the southern end of the Jordan valley, north of the Dead Sea, stands Jericho. This famous and ancient city grew up around a spring known since Old Testament times as Elisha's well. A story in 2 Kings chapter 2 verses 19 to 22 describes how the prophet

◁ Nebi Musa (which means the Prophet Moses in Arabic) is in the Jordan valley just south of Jericho. According to the Old Testament, Moses was not allowed to cross the river Jordan into Canaan. But the Muslim belief is that he traveled under the ground to a grave in the Promised Land. The picture shows the Muslim pilgrimage shrine for Moses' grave. Across the Judean Desert, in the background, is the Dead Sea.

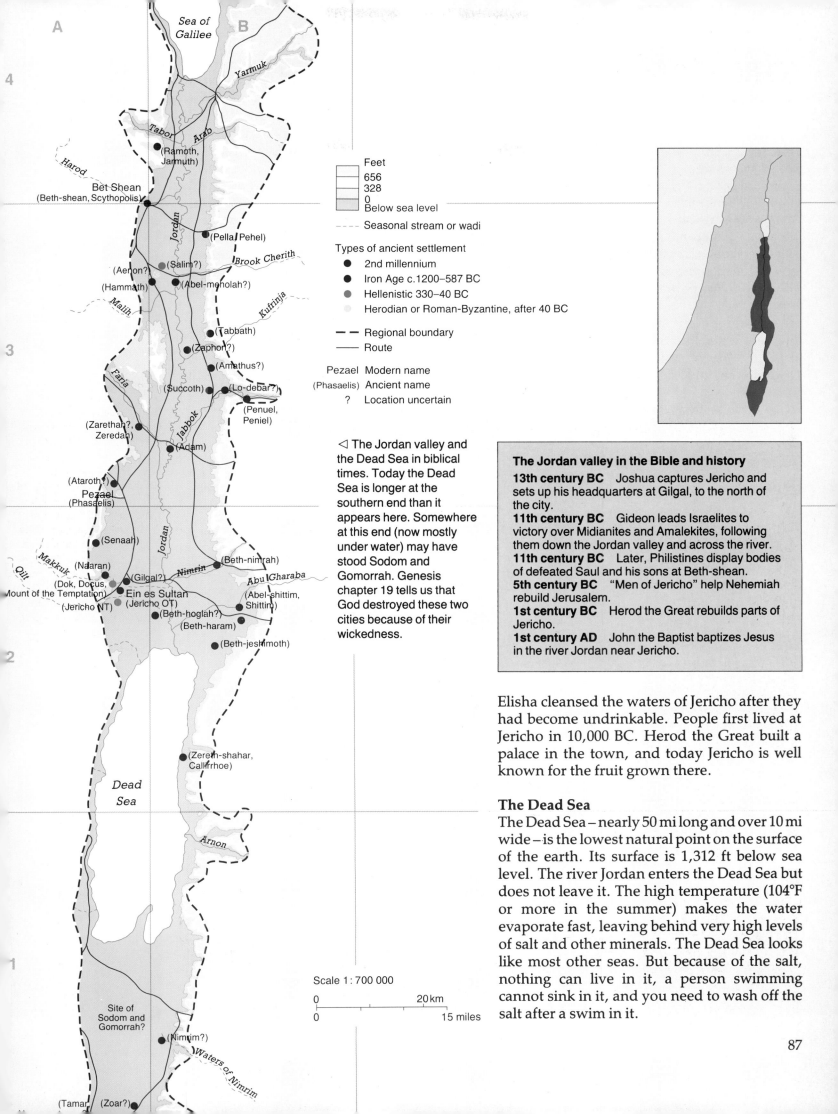

A · **B**

Sea of Galilee

4

Yarmuk

Tabor

Arab

Harod

(Ramoth, Jarmuth)

Bet Shean
(Beth-shean, Scythopolis)

Jordan

(Pella, Pehel)

(Aenon?) (Salim?) Brook Cherith

(Hammath) (Abel-meholah?)

Malih

Kufrinja

(Tabbath)

3

(Zaphon?)

Faria

(Amathus?)

(Succoth) (Lo-debar?)

Jabbok

(Zarethan?, Zeredah)

(Penuel, Peniel)

(Adam)

(Ataroth?)

Pezael
(Phasaelis)

Jordan

(Senaah)

Makkuk

(Naaran) Nimrin (Beth-nimrah)

Qilt (Gilgal?)

(Dok, Docus, Abu Gharaba
Mount of the Temptation)

Ein es Sultan

(Jericho OT) (Abel-shittim, Shittim)

(Jericho NT)

(Beth-hoglah?)

(Beth-haram)

(Beth-jeshimoth)

2

(Zereth-shahar, Callirrhoe)

Dead
Sea

Arnon

1

Site of
Sodom and
Gomorrah?

(Nimrim?)

(Tamar) (Zoar?)

Waters of Nimrim

Feet

656
328
0
Below sea level

\- - - Seasonal stream or wadi

Types of ancient settlement

● 2nd millennium
● Iron Age c.1200–587 BC
● Hellenistic 330–40 BC
○ Herodian or Roman-Byzantine, after 40 BC

— — Regional boundary
—— Route

Pezael Modern name
(Phasaelis) Ancient name
? Location uncertain

◁ The Jordan valley and the Dead Sea in biblical times. Today the Dead Sea is longer at the southern end than it appears here. Somewhere at this end (now mostly under water) may have stood Sodom and Gomorrah. Genesis chapter 19 tells us that God destroyed these two cities because of their wickedness.

Scale 1 : 700 000

0 ——————— 20km
0 ——————— 15 miles

The Jordan valley in the Bible and history

13th century BC Joshua captures Jericho and sets up his headquarters at Gilgal, to the north of the city.

11th century BC Gideon leads Israelites to victory over Midianites and Amalekites, following them down the Jordan valley and across the river.

11th century BC Later, Philistines display bodies of defeated Saul and his sons at Beth-shean.

5th century BC "Men of Jericho" help Nehemiah rebuild Jerusalem.

1st century BC Herod the Great rebuilds parts of Jericho.

1st century AD John the Baptist baptizes Jesus in the river Jordan near Jericho.

Elisha cleansed the waters of Jericho after they had become undrinkable. People first lived at Jericho in 10,000 BC. Herod the Great built a palace in the town, and today Jericho is well known for the fruit grown there.

The Dead Sea

The Dead Sea – nearly 50 mi long and over 10 mi wide – is the lowest natural point on the surface of the earth. Its surface is 1,312 ft below sea level. The river Jordan enters the Dead Sea but does not leave it. The high temperature (104°F or more in the summer) makes the water evaporate fast, leaving behind very high levels of salt and other minerals. The Dead Sea looks like most other seas. But because of the salt, nothing can live in it, a person swimming cannot sink in it, and you need to wash off the salt after a swim in it.

Jericho

People first lived at Jericho in about 10,000 BC, and a tower that was built in 7000 BC can still be seen there. Archaeologists have built up a detailed picture of Jericho's history, although traces of the city that Joshua captured have not been found. There are at least three Jerichos: the Old Testament site, the New Testament city farther south where the Wadi Qilt enters the Jordan valley, and modern Jericho. Herod built a palace in New Testament Jericho. A road cuts through part of the ancient site.

Beth-shean

The fortified city of Beth-shean was an important site guarding the entrance to the passage from the Jordan valley to the Valley of Jezreel. The Israelites were unable to capture Beth-shean when they first invaded Canaan; it became a Philistine city before David finally defeated the Philistines. By New Testament times it was a Greek city, named Scythopolis (meaning "city of the Scythians," a warlike people from the north). It was one of the decapolis (ten cities) mentioned in the New Testament.

◁ The Wadi Qilt is named after one of three springs that supplied New Testament Jericho with water. At the top of the picture you can see where the wadi (seasonal watercourse) enters the Jordan valley. During the winter the rains flood along its bottom.

▽ Site plan of Old Testament Jericho, showing how the modern road crosses part of the mound. Most of what can be seen today is much older than Old Testament times. The Neolithic tower, dating from 7000 BC, was built for defense against either enemies or floods.

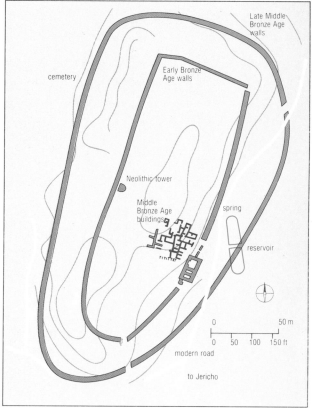

Late Middle Bronze Age walls

cemetery

Early Bronze Age walls

Neolithic tower

Middle Bronze Age buildings

spring

reservoir

| 0 | | | 50 m |
| 0 | 50 | 100 | 150 ft |

modern road

to Jericho

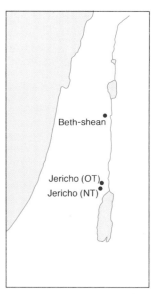

◁ View from the air of Beth-shean (the mound) and the theater at Scythopolis. Beth-shean is mentioned in Egyptian records that are older than the Bible, and people may have lived there from about 6000 BC. Since this photograph was taken, the area between the mound and the theater has been cleared of trees and excavated. This has revealed the remains of streets, fine public buildings, and mosaics dating from Roman and later times. The hills in the far distance are on the other (eastern) side of the river Jordan.

Beth-shean

Jericho (OT)
Jericho (NT)

TRANSJORDAN

Transjordan is the land to the east of the river Jordan. It covers almost as large an area as the Bible lands on the western side of the river. But it is not often mentioned in the Bible.

Bashan

The Old Testament sometimes mentions Bashan suggesting a place of smooth and possibly fertile land and strong, well-fed cattle. Bashan was a high and broad area to the northeast of the Sea of Galilee. Today it has some examples of the evergreen oak forests that once covered the land of the Bible, and herds of cows still eat its grass.

Ammon

About halfway between the Sea of Galilee and the Dead Sea was the kingdom of the Ammonites. When the Israelites entered the Promised Land some of them settled east of the river Jordan to the north of the Ammonites.

On becoming king, Saul had to face a threat from the king of Ammon against the Israelite town of Jabesh-gilead. He saved the town, and its people were very grateful. Years later, the men of Jabesh-gilead crossed the Jordan to the town of Beth-shean, where the Philistines had displayed the bodies of Saul and his sons, and they took them back to their town for a proper burial. The final battle between David and his rebel son Absalom also took place in a forest in the kingdom of Ammon.

Moab

The kingdom of Moab was roughly on the eastern side of the Dead Sea. Some of its

▷ Transjordan runs from north to south on the eastern side of the river Jordan. The rivers flowing westward into the Jordan valley or the Dead Sea divide Transjordan into sections. The main rivers are the Yarmuk, the Jabbok, and the Arnon. An important route, called the King's Highway in the Bible, goes through Edom and Moab.

◁ Remains of a shrine (place of worship) dedicated to the Greek god Pan at Baniyas, in northern Transjordan. One of the sources of the river Jordan starts nearby. The Bible lands came under Greek influence when the armies of Alexander the Great conquered the area in the 4th century BC. In New Testament times Baniyas was called Caesarea Philippi (the Caesarea in the territory of Philip). Here Jesus asked his followers who they thought he was, and Peter declared that he was the Messiah (God's special servant).

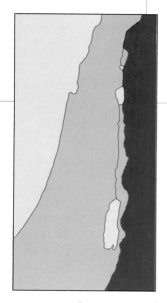

countryside was ideal for grazing sheep and good for growing food. In the story of Ruth, who came from Moab, the family of Naomi went from Bethlehem where there was no food to live in Moab where there was food.

In the time of David (10th century BC) and Omri (9th century BC) Israel ruled Moab. In Herod's reign the Jewish kingdom included Moab as far as the spectacular Arnon gorge through which the river Arnon flows into the Dead Sea.

Edom

The Edomites lived in the area roughly to the south of the Dead Sea. They, too, were ruled by David. But they got their revenge after the fall of Jerusalem in 587–586 BC when they occupied southern Judah.

Transjordan in the Bible and history

18th–17th centuries BC Jacob stops at the crossing of the river Jabbok on his way home after years of exile in Haran (Genesis chapter 32).

13th century BC Moses leads the Israelites through or round the territory of Edom and Moab toward the Promised Land.

11th century BC Saul saves the town of Jabesh-gilead from the king of Ammon.

10th century BC David rules Ammon, Moab, and Edom.

9th century BC Omri and Ahab rule Moab. Ahab fights the king of Syria at Ramoth-gilead.

8th century BC Amaziah, king of Judah, defeats the Edomites in the Valley of Salt.

6th century BC People of Judah flee to Ammon, Moab, and Edom when Nebuchadnezzar invades. The Edomites occupy southern Judah.

1st century AD John the Baptist is imprisoned in the fortress of Machaerus. Jesus teaches and heals east of the Sea of Galilee. At Caesarea Philippi (Baniyas), Peter says Jesus is the Messiah.

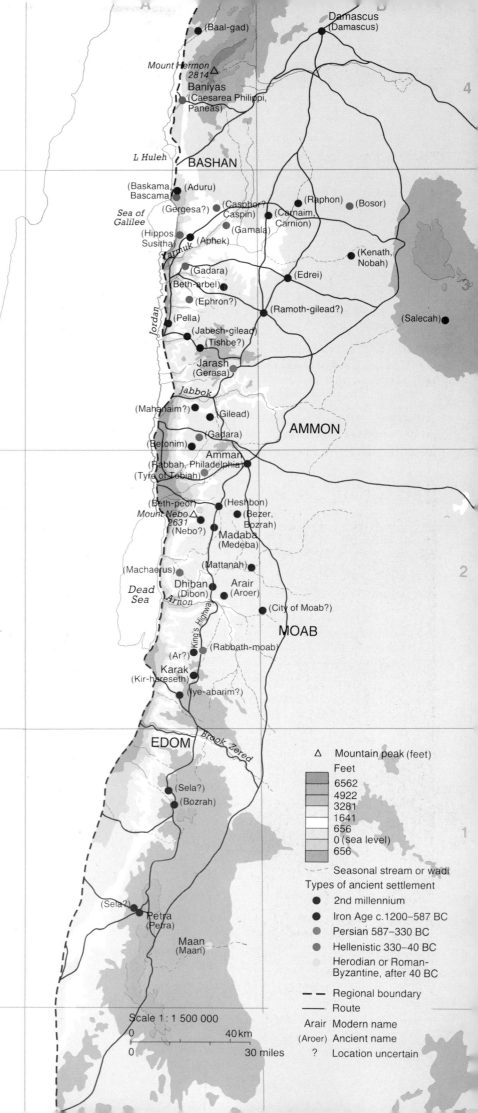

Damascus
(Damascus)

(Baal-gad)

Mount Hermon △
2814

Baniyas
(Caesarea Philippi,
Paneas)

L Huleh

BASHAN

(Baskama,
Bascama)   (Aduru)

Sea of   (Gergesa?)   (Casphor?
Galilee   Caspin)   (Carnaim,   (Raphon)   (Bosor)
                                Carnion)

(Gamala)

(Hippos,
Susitha)   (Aphek)

Yarmuk   (Gadara)   (Kenath,
Beth-arbel)   (Edrei)   Nobah)

(Ephron?)   (Ramoth-gilead?)   (Salecah)

(Pella)

(Jabesh-gilead)
(Tishbe?)

Jarash
(Gerasa)

Jabbok

(Mahanaim?)   (Gilead)

(Gadara)   AMMON

(Betonim)   Amman
(Rabbah, Philadelphia)
(Tyre of Tobiah)

(Beth-peor)   (Heshbon)
Mount Nebo △   (Bezer,
2631   Bozrah)
(Nebo?)   Madaba
            (Medeba)

(Machaerus)   (Mattanah)

Dead   Dhiban   Arair
Sea   (Dibon)   (Aroer)

Arnon   (City of Moab?)

King's Highway   MOAB

(Ar?)   (Rabbath-moab)

Karak
(Kir-hareseth)

(Iye-abarim?)

Brook Zered

EDOM

(Sela?)

(Bozrah)

(Sela?)   Petra
           (Petra)

Maan
(Maan)

△   Mountain peak (feet)
Feet
6562
4922
3281
1641
656
0 (sea level)
656

– – –   Seasonal stream or wadi

Types of ancient settlement
●   2nd millennium
●   Iron Age c.1200–587 BC
●   Persian 587–330 BC
●   Hellenistic 330–40 BC
     Herodian or Roman-
     Byzantine, after 40 BC

– –   Regional boundary
——   Route
Arair   Modern name
(Aroer) Ancient name
?   Location uncertain

Scale 1 : 1 500 000
0   40 km
0   30 miles

GLOSSARY

Aramaic A language belonging to the same family as Hebrew that became the official language of the Persian Empire and was used among Jews from 540 BC. Aramaic was the language spoken by Jesus.

Ark of the Covenant A box in which were kept the Ten Commandments written on two tablets of stone. The Ark was also carried by the Israelites when they went into battle.

Byzantine Belonging to the Eastern Roman Empire whose capital was Byzantium (also known as Constantinople), the present-day Istanbul in Turkey. For the land of the Bible, the Byzantine period lasted from the 4th to the 7th centuries AD.

convert To persuade a person to change from one religion to another.

Covenant A special agreement between two parties. In the Bible, God made a covenant with the Israelites. They were to be God's special people, but in return they were to worship him and obey his laws.

Disciple A follower or pupil. The early followers of Jesus were called disciples, and an inner group was known as the Twelve Disciples.

Gospel A shortened form of older English "Good spell" (news), which translated the Greek word *euangellion* (good news) in the New Testament. The message of Jesus is described as *euangellion*, and the four accounts of the life of Jesus are called in Greek the *euangellion* according to Matthew and so on.

Hanukkah A Hebrew word meaning dedication. It is a religious festival held each year by Jews and remembers that Judas Maccabeus rededicated the temple in 164 BC after a foreign invader had erected in it the image of a false god.

Hasmonean A general name for the leaders of the Jews from the time of Judas Maccabeus – the hammer (167 BC) – until the Romans became rulers of Judea in 63 BC.

Hebrew The language spoken and written by the Israelites. When Judah became part of the Persian Empire in 540 BC, Aramaic began to be spoken and written alongside Hebrew.

Hellenistic Relating to the Greek-speaking civilization that spread through many lands of the Eastern Mediterranean and beyond following the conquests of Alexander the Great in the 4th century BC.

Herodian During the period of the Roman-backed king of Judea Herod the Great (37 to 4 BC) and of his sons (to about AD 40).

Hyksos An Egyptian name meaning rulers of foreign lands, and referring to non-Egyptians who ruled part of Egypt from about 1720 to 1567 BC. During their rule people such as Abraham and Jacob were able to enter and settle in Egypt.

Iron Age The period of human culture when people learned to smelt iron and to make and use iron tools. It dates from about 1600 to 1000 BC.

Maccabean Having to do with Judas Maccabeus or his successors in the 2nd century BC.

Messiah A Hebrew and Aramaic word meaning anointed. The word became the title for a future deliverer or deliverers of Israel whom God would use to establish his rule in the world.

miracle A happening for which there is no natural explanation. Jesus performed a miracle when he fed 5,000 people from two loaves and five small fishes.

Muslim A follower of the religion of Islam. This religion came into being in the 7th century AD through the prophet Muhammad.

Passover A major religious festival of the Jews, which is held once a year and reminds them how they escaped from being slaves in Egypt.

Persian (period) Relating to the civilization of peoples from Persia (present-day Iran) from the time of Darius in 495 BC to about a century after Alexander the Great, who died in 323 BC.

Pharaoh An Egyptian word meaning great house, but used in the Bible to refer to a king of Egypt.

prophet, prophetess A man or woman called to be a special messenger of God and to declare what God is about to do.

route The course of a journey or a travelway. In Biblical times there were no roads but tracks and pathways.

Sabbath A Hebrew word meaning a day on which no work is to be done. In Israel, this was the seventh day (Saturday).

Sanhedrin A court of justice in Jerusalem.

tell An Arabic word meaning the hill or mound of an ancient city.

tribute A payment usually in gold and silver by a defeated king to his victor.

FURTHER READING

Denis Baly, *Basic Biblical Geography* (Augsburg Fortress) 1987

F. F. Bruce, *New Testament History* (Doubleday), 1972

John and Kathleen Court, *The New Testament World* (Prentice Hall) 1990

Clifford M. Jones, *Old Testament Illustrations* (Cambridge), 1971

Clifford M. Jones, *New Testament Illustrations* (Cambridge), 1966

Kathleen Kenyon and P. R. Moorey, *The Bible and Recent Archaeology* (Westminster/John Knox), 1987

Amihai Mazar, *Archaeology of the Land of the Bible* (Doubleday), 1990

P. R. Moorey, *The Biblical Lands: The Making of the Past* (Bedrick, Peter), 1991

John Rogerson and Philip Davies, *The Old Testament World* (Prentice Hall), 1989

Hershel Shanks, *Ancient Israel* (Prentice Hall), 1988

GAZETTEER

The gazetteer lists places and features, such as rivers or mountains, found on the maps. Each has a separate entry including a page and grid reference number. For example:

Abronah 69 C3

Where a place also has a modern name form this name is added to the entry before the reference number. For example:

Adoraim (Dura) 63 B3

All features are shown in italic type. For example:

Alexander, r. 57 C3

A letter after the feature describes the kind of feature:

d. district; *f.* feature; *r.* river

Abdon (Avdon) 73 A4
Abel-beth-maacah 73 D5
Abel-meholah 87 B3
Abel-shittim 87 B2
Abronah 69 C3
Abu Ghosh *see* Emmaus
Accaron 57 C2
Acco (Akko) 53 B3, 73 A3
Achshaph 73 A2
Achshaph 73 A3
Achzib 61 B2
Achzib 73 A4
Acraba (Aqraba) 77 C2
Adadah 69 C5
Adam 87 B3
Adamah 73 C2
Adamah 73 D3
Adami-nekeb 73 C2
Adasa 81 C3
Adithaim 77 B1
Adora 63 B3
Adoraim (Dura) 63 B3
Adullam 61 C2
Aduru 91 A3
Aenon 87 B3
Afeq *see* Aphek
Afula *see* Ophrah
Ahlab 73 B5
Ai 77 C1
Aialon 77 C1
Aiath 77 C1
Aija 77 C1
Aijalon 61 C4
Aila 69 D3
Ain 63 A2
Ain Karem *see* Beth-haccherem
Akko *see* Acco
Akrabatta 77 C2
Alemeth 81 D2
Alexander, r. 57 C3
Almon 81 D2
Amathus 87 B3
Amman *see* Rabbah
Ammathus 73 D2
Ammon, d. 91 B3
Anab 63 A2
Anaharath 73 C1
Ananiah 81 D2
Anata *see* Anathoth
Anathoth (Anata) 81 D2
Anim 63 B2
Aphairema 77 C1

Aphek 57 C3
Aphek 57 C3
Aphek 91 A3
Aphek (Afeq) 73 A3
Aphekah 63 B3
Aphekah 63 B3
Aphik 73 A3
Apollonia 57 B3
Aqaba *see* Elath
Aqraba *see* Acraba
Ar 91 A2
Arab 63 B3
Arabah, The, f. 69 D4
Arad (Arad) 69 D5
Arad (Tel Malhata) 69 C5
Arair *see* Aroer
Arbela 73 C2
Arimathea 77 B2
Arnon, r. 53 B2, 87 B1, 91 A2
Aroer 69 C5
Aroer 91 A2
Arubboth 57 C4
Arumah 77 C2
Ascalon 57 B1
Ashdod (Ashdod) 53 A2, 57 B2
Ashkelon (Ashqelon) 53 A2, 57 B1
Ashnah 61 B2
Ashnah 61 C3
Ashqelon *see* Ashkelon
Asor (Azor) 57 B3
Ataroth 77 B3
Ataroth 87 A3
Ataroth-addar 81 C3
Athlit (Atlit) 57 C5
Atlit *see* Athlit
Avdon *see* Abdon
Ayyalon, r. 57 C2
Azekah 61 B3
Azmaveth (Hisma) 81 D2
Azmon 69 C4
Aznoth-tabor 73 C2
Azor *see* Asor
Azotus 57 B2
Azzah 77 B3

Baal-gad 91 A4
Baal-hazor 77 C1
Baal-perazim 81 C1
Baal-shalishah 77 B2
Baalah 81 A2
Baalath 57 B2
Bahurim 81 D2
Baniyas *see* Caesarea Philippi
Bascama 91 A3
Bashan, d. 91 A4
Baskama 91 A3
Beer 61 B3
Beer 73 D1
Beer-sheba (Beersheba) 53 A2, 69 C5
Beer-sheba, r. 69 C5/D5
Beeroth (Bira) 81 C3
Beeroth 69 C4
Beeroth 81 C2
Beersheba *see* Beer-sheba
Beerzeth 77 B1
Beit Jann *see* Beth-dagon
Beitin *see* Bethel
Bene-berak 57 B3
Bene-jaakan 69 C4
Berea 77 C3
Besor, r. 53 A2, 69 C5
Bet Shean *see* Beth-shean
Bet Dagan *see* Beth-dagon
Bet ha-Emeq *see* Beth-emek
Bet Shemesh *see* Beth-shemesh
Beten 73 A2
Beth-anath 73 C5
Beth-anath (Bina) 73 B3
Beth-anath 73 C2

Beth-anoth 63 B3
Beth-arabah 63 D5
Beth-arbel 91 A3
Beth-aven 81 D3
Beth-basi 63 B4
Beth-dagon (Bet Dagan) 57 B2
Beth-dagon (Beit Jann) 73 C3
Beth-dagon 77 C2
Beth-eked 77 B4
Beth-emek (Bet ha-Emeq) 73 A3
Beth-ezel 63 A3
Beth-haccherem (Ain Karem) 81 B2
Beth-haccherem (Majd el Kurum) 73 B3
Beth-haccherem (Ramat Rahel) 81 C1
Beth-haggan (Jenin) 77 C4
Beth-hanan 81 B3
Beth-haram 87 B2
Beth-hoglah 87 B2
Beth-jeshimoth 87 B2
Beth-nimrah 87 B2
Beth-omri 77 B3
Beth-peor 91 A2
Beth-shean (Bet Shean) 53 B3, 87 A4
Beth-shemesh (Bet Shemesh) 61 B3
Beth-shemesh 73 B4
Beth-shemesh 73 D2
Beth-shittah 77 C5
Beth-tappuah (Taffuh) 63 B3
Beth-zaith 63 B4
Beth-zechariah 63 B4
Beth-zita 63 B4
Beth-zur 63 B4
Bethany (Eizariya) 81 D2
Bethel Hills 77 B1
Bethel (Beitin) 77 B1
Bethir 81 B1
Bethlehem (Bethlehem) 53 B2, 63 B4
Bethlehem 73 B2
Bethphage 81 C2
Bethsaida 73 D3
Bethsaida 73 D3
Bethsura 63 B4
Bethuel 63 A2
Bethul 63 A2
Bethul 63 B2
Betonim 91 A3
Bezek 77 A1
Bezek 77 C4
Bezer 91 A2
Bileam 77 C4
Bina *see* Beth-anath
Bira *see* Beeroth
Bosor 91 B3
Bozkath 61 B2
Bozrah 91 A1
Bozrah 91 A2

Cabbon 61 B2
Cabul 73 B3
Cadasa 73 D4
Caesarea 57 C4
Caesarea Philippi (Baniyas) 91 A4
Callirrhoe 87 B2
Cana 73 B2
Cana (Kafr Kanna) 73 C2
Capernaum 73 D3
Capharsalama 81 C3
Carmel 63 B3
Carmel, Mt 53 B3, 57 C5, 77 B6
Carnaim 91 B3
Carnion 91 B3
Casphor 91 A3
Caspin 91 A3
Chephar-ammoni 77 C1

Chephirah 81 B2
Chesalon (Kesalon) 81 A2
Chesulloth 73 B2
Chinnereth 73 D3
Chinneroth 73 D3
Chitlish 61 A2
Chorazin 73 D3
City of Moab 91 B2
City of Salt 63 C4
City of Salt 63 C4
Cozeba 63 B4

Dabbesheth 77 B5
Daberath 73 C2
Damascus (Damascus) 91 B4
Dan (Dan) 53 B4, 73 D5
Dannah 63 B2
Daphne 73 D5
Dead Sea 53 B2, 63 C3, 87 A2, 91 A2
Debir 61 B1
Debir 63 B3
Dhiban *see* Dibon
Dibon 91 A2
Dilean 61 A2
Dimnah 73 B2
Dimona *see* Dimonah
Dimonah (Dimona) 69 D5
Diocaesarea 73 B2
Docus 87 A2
Dok 87 A2
Dophkah 69 B2
Dor (Dor) 57 C4
Dothan 77 B4
Dumah 63 A3
Dura *see* Adoraim

East Samaria Hills 77 C2
Eben-ezer 77 C1
Eben-ezer (Sarta) 57 C3
Ebenezer 77 A2
Edom, d. 91 A1
Edrei 91 B3
Eglon 61 A2
Eglon 61 B1
Ein es Sultan *see* Jericho
Ein el-Ghuweir *see* Nibshan
Eizariya *see* Bethany
Ekron 57 C2
Elah, r. 61 B3
Elam 61 B2
Elasa 77 B1
Elath (Aqaba) 69 D3
El Jib *see* Gibeon
Elon 61 B3
Elon 61 C4
Eltekeh 57 C2
Emmaus 61 B4
Emmaus (Abu Ghosh) 81 B2
Emmaus (Moza) 81 B2
Emmaus (Qubeibah) 81 B2
En-dor (En-dor) 73 C1
En-eglaim 63 C4
En-gannim 61 B3
En-gedi (En-gedi) 63 C3
En-haddah 73 C2
En-hazor 73 C4
En-Naqura 77 B3
En-rimmon 63 A2
En-shemesh 81 D2
En-tappuah 77 B2
Enadab 81 A1
Ephrath 63 B4
Ephron 91 A3
es-Samu *see* Eshtemoa
Eshan 63 A3
Eshtaol (Eshtaol) 61 C3
Eshtemoa (es-Samu) 63 B2
Etam 63 B4
Ether 61 B2
Evron 73 A4
Ezion-geber 69 C3

Faria, r. 77 C3, 87 A3

Gaash 77 B1
Gabara 73 C3
Gabatha 73 B2
Gadara 91 A3
Gadara 91 A3
Galilee, Sea of 53 B3, 73 D2, 87 B4, 91 A3
Gallim 81 C2
Gamala 91 A3
Gath 57 C2
Gath 73 B3
Gath-hepher 73 B2
Gath-rimmon 57 B3
Gaza (Gaza) 53 A2, 57 A1
Gazara 61 B4
Geba 77 B3
Geba 77 C2
Geba 81 D3
Gebel Halal, Mt (Sinai, Mt) 69 B4
Gebel Musa, Mt (Sinai, Mt) 69 B2
Gebel Serbal, Mt (Sinai, Mt) 69 B2
(Gedera) 53 A2
Gederah 61 B3
Gederah 81 A3
Gederoth 61 B3
Gederothaim 61 B3
Gedor 63 B4
Gerasa 77 C2
Gerasa (Jarash) 91 A3
Gergesa 91 A3
Gerizim, Mt 53 B3, 77 C3
Gezer (Gezer) 61 B4
Gibbethon 57 B2
Gibe-ah 63 B4
Gibeah 81 C2
Gibeah 81 C3
Gibeon (El Jib) 81 C3
Gilboa 77 C4
Gilboa, Mt 77 C5
Gilboa, Mts 53 B3
Gilead 91 A3
Gilgal 57 C3
Gilgal 77 B2
Gilgal 87 A2
Gimzo 57 C2
Ginae 77 C4
Gischala 73 C4
Gittaim 57 C2
Gomorrah 87 A1
Gophna 77 B1
Goshen 61 B1
Goshen 63 A2
Gurbaal 63 A1

(Hadera) 53 A3
Hadera, r. 57 C4, 77 B4
Hadid (Hadid) 57 C2
Haifa (Haifa) 53 A3, 57 C5
Halhul 63 B3
Hammath 73 D2
Hammath 87 B3
Hammon 73 A4
Hannathon 73 B2
Hapharaim 77 B5
Harim 61 B2
Harod 77 C5
Harod 81 D1
Harod, r. 77 C5, 87 A4
Harosheth-ha-goiim 77 B6
Hazazon-tamar 63 C3
Hazazon-tamar 87 A1
Hazeroth 77 C3
Hazor 81 C2
Hazor (Hazor) 73 D4
Hebron Hills 53 B2, 63 B3
Hebron (Hebron) 53 B2, 63 B3
Helkath 73 A2

INDEX

Page numbers in *italics* refer to illustrations or their captions